50 Fashion Ideas
You Really
Need to Know
Jessica Bumpus

greenfinch

Contents

Introduction

My early interest in fashion comes from the dressing-up box; the shoes and handbags I plucked from the bottom of my mum's wardrobe; corners of the high-school library, poring over copies of *Vogue* with my friends; and the flashes of the catwalk I got to see while watching *The Clothes Show*, a television programme that aired in the United Kingdom during the 1990s. Later on, of course, like many others, I faithfully tuned in to watch *Sex and the City*.

The thing I probably love most about fashion, though, is its history, and there are so many eras I wish I could have been alive in to experience it. That's one of the reasons this book has been so fascinating to write, allowing me to dip back into the past and, for a moment or two, indulge this dream.

For some, fashion is simply about the practicalities of getting dressed, whereas, for others, it is all wrapped up in fantasy. Both views are valid – and central to the ideas explored in this book. Admittedly, it was not easy to pick just 50 big ideas, partly because the world of fashion is forever changing, even more so today. But there are some fundamentals. Those that have been pinpointed aim to provide a beneficial overview in terms of where fashion has come from and why; the foundations of the way the industry works and is evolving; the meanings attached to and associated with certain garments; and key references that designers use time and again in their collections (clearly, there are reasons), plus how to spot them.

Ideally, the book will serve as a jumping off point for anything you find especially interesting, be it the technical wizardry of the bias cut (which I personally found among the most enjoyable chapters to write!), the discovery of a certain designer (there are so many more than this book has been able to cover) or the role that cinema played initially in setting the trends.

Jessica Bumpus

01 Haute Couture

The one-off garments created especially for clients are regarded as the highest pinnacle of design and creativity in the world of fashion today. Such pieces – termed 'haute couture' – are showcased in Paris twice a year (January and July), where avant-garde and magical constructs are seen alongside precision tailoring and inconspicuous ultra-luxury for designs that only select clients will ever likely wear. The genre is often thought of as being the original sustainable way to design – with its focus on quality, forever wear and made to order, there is very little waste.

Today, those lucky enough to be a part of couture's lofty heights are an elusive and elite few, but this has not always been so, as there was a time when couture presentations were standard shopping expeditions for upper-class women. In recent years, it is thought that only 4,000 couture clients exist worldwide, a number that has declined significantly from an estimated 20,000 in 1950. Why? Because couture is not cheap; it is artistry. Pieces typically cost upwards of hundreds of thousands of pounds. And there is a reason for this.

Couture, a French word, means 'sewing' or 'needlework', all of which is done by hand and, in this instance, by many skilled hands – *petites mains* – who create collections brimming with technical savoir-faire. As an industry, it relies on specialists: those who make buttons, gloves, trimmings and millinery to a high level of craftsmanship. It is labour intensive and garments are made up to precise measurements

When is couture season?

Couture shows, lasting four or five days, take place ahead of the ready-to-wear shows by about a month or two. The January shows present the spring/summer collections and the July shows present the autumn/winter collections. In ready-to-wear, the February/March shows present the autumn/winter collections and the September/October shows present the spring/summer collections. The two work to different timelines.

and after many fittings with a client so that each piece is perfect. More importantly, each piece is unique and it is this fundamental difference that sets couture apart from ready-to-wear.

The rules

Strict rules and regulations apply in order for an haute couture house (*maison*) to gain its status:

• Members must create made-to-order garments in an atelier that has at least 15 full-time staff, plus 20 full-time technical workers in one of their ateliers.

• Collections must have a minimum of 50 original designs that include day and evening looks, to be presented to the public and made for private clients.

• Each piece should undergo more than one fitting.

• Each season, guest designers are invited to show. Should they be invited four times in a row, they are then eligible to become members.

Charles Frederick Worth

British-born Charles Frederick Worth is widely regarded as the grandfather of French couture. He made a name in retail, apprenticing at the London draper's Swan & Edgar during a period of growth in the mid-19th century, when shopping started to become a new social and leisure activity for middle-class and aristocratic women, and later at Lewis and Allenby, a silk haberdashery to Queen Victoria.

Moving to Paris in 1845, he worked at a premium drapery shop, where he helped to establish a dressmaking department. He received great recognition and his prize-winning designs were displayed at London's Great Exhibition, in 1851, and the Exposition Universelle in Paris, 1855. His reputation soon spread, his style recognizable for its lavish fabrics and trimmings, daring nature and technique, and historic elements. By 1858, he had established his own dressmaking business at 7 rue de la Paix, in partnership with Otto Bobergh, and became a favourite of the Empress Eugénie, wife of Napoleon III. He created her state and eveningwear, which made him and his designs very well known and highly covetable.

Worth promoted himself as a tastemaker. Clients had to come to him, rather than the other way round, and he instituted a system by which they selected from designs in his current range that would then be made up to their measurements. This is typical of how a couture house operates still, though clients may be able to request elements of modification, such as colour.

Chambre Syndicale de la Haute Couture

Couture is a preserve of the French – France has been a leader in fashion since King Louis XIV came to the throne in the 17th century, and recognized the power of its influence. It was in 1868 that a union of dress designers called the Chambre Syndicale de la Confectionneurs et des Tailleurs pour Dame was formed with the aim to safeguard the designers, manufacturers and tailors of women's clothing from having their designs copied. By 1910, it had become the Chambre de la Couture Parisienne, which comprised couturiers alone. The idea was that it would promote French fashion houses overseas, where they would also show their collections. This became important after World War II as America started to develop as a hub for mass manufacture while Paris established itself as the centre of couture.

On 23 January 1945, the organization became the Chambre Syndicale de la Haute Couture; that same year, the term 'haute couture' became a legally protected term, awarded only by a commission appointed by the Ministry of Industry. The Chambre is part of the Fédération de la Haute Couture et de la Mode, which is the governing body of fashion in France.

In an attempt to court its pre-war international clientele, in 1945, the Chambre Syndicale de la Couture organized a travelling show, or theatre of fashion, to be held in Barcelona, Paris, London, Copenhagen, Stockholm, Vienna, New York and San Francisco. Big houses of the day presented daywear collections on miniature wire dress models to imaginative and fantastical effect. Despite this, the allure of ready-to-wear, which had emerged at the start of the 20th century, started to have a detrimental impact on the category. It is thought there was a total of 106 houses in 1946, which dwindled to 60 in 1952 and 36 in 1958. By 1970, there were only 19.

In recent years, the relevance of haute couture has been called into question, since it is estimated that there are just 10 official French couture houses remaining. But with each season the Chambre invites 'Guest Members' and 'Corresponding Members' (leading fashion brands from around the world) to join the spectacle. The move has introduced an exciting blend of new ideas and a slightly more democratic approach to the world of couture. Guest Members include Imane Ayissi, Ronald van der Kemp and Robert Wun, and Corresponding Members, Fendi, Elie Saab and Giorgio Armani.

Italian couture

In Italy, members of the bourgeoisie were dressed by the couturiers of Rome, Venice, Turin and Florence. Typically, however, they were led by what the French couturiers were doing, observed the fashion editor Anna Gloria Forti. In 1935, the Ente Nazionale della Moda (Italian Fashion Society) was created and, at the request of Benito Mussolini, used home-grown ideas and materials, which led to the development of a highly skilled artisan industry (though wartime rationing played a role). After the war, Giovanni Battista Giorgini was employed by American department stores to select and buy Italian-made products. He came up with the idea to organize a group fashion show, to which the most important US buyers came. Held at Villa Torrigiani in Florence on 12 February 1951, it was a success – the next one would take place in a larger, more esteemed setting, the Pitti Palace.

During the 1960s, Valentino and Krizia were notable stars on the rise as result of Giorgini's work, though some names did choose to present their collections in Paris. This, paired with the rise of ready-to-wear, signalled a decline for the Pitti show, after which Rome became Italy's official home of haute couture, largely owing, it's noted, to its connections with movie stars.

The condensed idea
Where it all began

02 Uniforms

A typical dictionary definition of the word 'uniform' will describe a set of the same, distinctive clothes worn by members of the same organization. Almost all of us will wear a uniform of a sorts at some point in our lives.

Typical examples include the school uniforms worn in certain parts of the world, such as the United Kingdom, China, Australia and Japan, and specialized uniforms for the army, for sports, as livery, and as workwear for certain professions. We see uniforms every day; they are signifiers of social order. But they are also signifiers about ourselves – beyond the required uniforms of life, we dress ourselves in ways that serve to give us some form of identity.

In terms of fashion, uniforms are a means of direct communication, giving immediate visual cues. They denote the status or trade of an individual, perhaps their age or qualifications, sometimes their class, or their religious or political beliefs. They can give an indication of space and time – whether someone is off-duty or engaged in a leisure activity. They help us navigate the world around us.

Hierarchy in uniform

Hierarchical dress has long existed. One suggestion is that it originated in antiquity as the costumes of bodyguards of monarchs. Certainly, the ancient Greek and Roman armies wore uniforms, just as armed forces have for centuries throughout the world. Even earlier than this, during ancient Egyptian times, lower classes and slaves in the palaces would go almost without clothes as if wearing them was a form of class distinction.

Similarly, the clothes of peasants during the Middle Ages did not convey the extravagance and wealth of those worn in court circles. A sumptuary law passed in England in 1363, for example, prohibited different sections of society from wearing clothing that was higher in value than a specified amount or made from certain luxurious fabrics. Such laws were prevalent across Europe during the medieval period and are thought not to have been uncommon in the ancient world too. In Italy, between the years 1200 and 1500, 300 sumptuary laws were enacted.

Blue collar versus white collar

The terms 'blue collar' and 'white collar' have come into popular use to describe the type of work a person does. Blue collar refers to manual labour – owing to the uniform typically being a darker colour – and white collar refers to an office job, where workers are typically seen wearing white shirts.

During the first half of the 16th century, clothes of the upper classes in Europe were bright in colour – red was a popular choice – and royal garments were typically encrusted with diamonds, rubies and pearls. Such conspicuous clothing was sure to ruffle some feathers. Among the demands of the German Peasants' War (1524–25) was reportedly that they, too, should be able to wear red clothes.

The ruff was the mark of aristocratic privilege during Elizabethan times (1558–1603) and ornate dress has generally continued to signify a wealthy status. In recent years, the term 'quiet luxury', has come into usage – largely thanks to the popular television show *Succession*. It refers to the tendency for people with wealth to dress in an understated way, in garments of the very highest quality.

From work to wardrobe

Uniforms are designed for practical purposes, often reflected in the choice of durable and/or comfortable fabric in colours best suited to their purpose. Over the years several staples have transitioned over into fashion. It is from naval uniforms, for example, that we have the striped breton top – a signature design from French fashion designer Jean Paul Gaultier and a hallmark of Coco Chanel's personal style. Its design meant that sailors who fell overboard could be easily spotted. The ever-popular trench coat and pea coat both have military origins and have become enduring, classic, go-to items regardless of what is or isn't trending.

The jumpsuit was originally introduced for pilots and parachutists and, later known as a boilersuit, used by mechanics and labourers as a practical all-in-one set of overalls. It is claimed that its first appearance

Style uniforms

In contemporary fashion, the idea of a uniform has often meant not having to think too much about what you will wear. English fashion designer Phoebe Philo's oversized white shirts, for example, became a go-to uniform for women during her tenure at Céline. The look was both smart and intellectual but a little bit creative. The term is often applied to a fail-safe look or something – for example, the combination of blazer, jeans, ballet pumps – someone routinely wears.

in the pages of *Vogue* was in 1964, a design by Yves Saint Laurent, and it remains a staple of the catwalk. It can be seen everywhere today – from offices to mother-and-toddler groups. It is interesting that the items that began life as uniforms have typically carried a sense of that with them.

Style tribes

Style tribes are groups of people who dress in a distinctive manner to show that they have membership to a certain group or subculture. In the 1950s and 1960s in the United Kingdom, Mods – a term derived from the word 'Modernist' – wore long parkas with US Air Force emblems over Italian-style suits, and rode scooters. This was their uniform in the face of Rockers, a different style tribe whose members wore tight jeans and leather biker jackets. The Sloane Ranger was a term used to describe the style uniform of women who lived in the expensive areas of West London, such as King's Road and Sloane Square. They wore preppy styles, including headbands and pearls.

Designer uniforms

The concept of the 'uniform' has provided various designers with inspiration for their collections. The American, Thom Browne, has regularly referenced traditional tailoring intended for the office and mixed it with school uniform elements to create his signature style. While Swiss luxury fashion house Vetements (at the time headed up

Acts of rebellion

Just as uniforms can work to create a streamlined society, signalling a sense of order through dress, they can also invite disorder and rebellion, the rise of individuality and personalization. Faux militaria became popular during the 1960s, as popularized by the release of The Beatles' album *Sgt. Pepper's Lonely Hearts Club Band* (1967).

by Demna Gvasalia) explored social tropes in society from commuters to punks for its autumn/winter 2017 catwalk. Beyond their collections, designers often create uniforms for hotels and restaurants or airlines. American designer Zac Posen created uniforms for Delta Air Lines staff in 2016, while Ralph Lauren, Armani and Christian Louboutin have all been involved in creating outfits for the Olympics.

Designers themselves have uniforms. At the end of a fashion show, when they take their bows, the audience will see them typically dressed down in a pair of jeans and a sweatshirt or dressed all in black – clothing that is usually in stark contrast to their collection and bringing with it an air of cool creativity.

The condensed idea
Social signifiers that keep order and convey identity

03 Menswear

There is a general conception in fashion that womenswear is more exciting than menswear, that it is more elaborate and that designers can have more fun designing it. It is true that womenswear shows tend to garner more press coverage and that, on red carpets, it is the women who are mostly listed in the best dressed lists (although this has begun to change in recent years).

Historically, however, this has not always been the case. For a time, menswear and womenswear, especially in the Western world, were both largely similar and based on slightly modified versions of the same garments. It is largely from menswear that womenswear has borrowed over the years – and, hence, transferred the freedoms, powers and associations that come with it.

Wigs, high heels and make-up have all been the preserve of men in various cultures at one point or another. Royal courts show both kings and queens in extravagant dress, costume-like by today's standards. Among womenswear, modern iterations of such ornate gowns still exist – in wedding gowns, for example – but in menswear, there is no equivalent. Along the way, something happened.

The Great Masculine Renunciation

In what British psychoanalyst and psychologist John Carl Flügel coined The Great Masculine Renunciation at the end of the 18th century, menswear took a turn for sobriety. In his book *The Psychology of Clothes* (1930), he explained that men had handed over their right to wear colour and ornamentation to women in a bid to be more useful in society, rather than beautiful. Their attire became pragmatic and precise, with no room for whimsy of centuries past. The move was linked to The Enlightenment of the 17th and 18th centuries, a period during which focus was placed on reason and science.

In the 18th and 19th centuries, the term 'dandy' began to be in use (the 'macaroni' had been its precursor). Epitomized by George Bryan Brummell, known as Beau Brummell, a dandy was a fashionable man, who cared about the perfection of his appearance, which was to be neat, exacting. The dandy was not an overdressed man, as has sometimes been assumed, but he did care about his appearance and,

Suiting up

In the late 12th century, plate armour is noted as being revolutionary in the advance of fashion in Europe. It not only protected the body, but it enhanced and articulated it, showed it off and explored new fitting lines to the torso – a significant development at a time when clothing was still largely loose and draped. Most interesting is that a linen undergarment was worn under the armour. As such, suggests historian Anne Hollander, linen armourers were essentially the first tailors of Europe.

as some have said, was a narcissist. He wore top hats and upright collars and wore mostly black. The English poet Lord Byron and Irish playwright Oscar Wilde are also considered dandies.

American historian Anne Hollander notes that the modern masculine image was mostly in place by 1820 and has only slightly modified since. Modern suits started life in the late 17th century with a loose-fitting, buttoned coat replacing the doublet – a type of fitted jacket – and breeches still worn with the addition of a waistcoat. Essentially, this was the forerunner of the three-piece suit.

Though regularly worn by women today, the suit is a particular mainstay of the male wardrobe. It signifies adulthood, the world of work and professionalism, sophistication and responsibility. Its most famous flashy version is the tuxedo, a favourite of film characters such as James Bond, Jay Gatsby and Bruce Wayne. The tuxedo, a semi-formal dinner jacket with silk lapels, took its name from the Tuxedo Club,

> Red-carpet dressing has brought new ideas around how men can approach suiting in more individual ways.
> Simon Chilvers, *The Guardian*

which opened in 1886 in Tuxedo Park, Orange County, New York, in the United States. Around the same time, a similar dress coat without tails was popular in the United Kingdom. It has varied from being single- and double-breasted, but overall, just like a suit, represents a confidence and maturity of masculinity.

In January and June each year, menswear fashion weeks take place in Paris and Milan, but it is Pitti Uomo, in Florence, which began in 1972, that becomes the epicentre of menswear twice a year. Starting out as a way to exhibit Italian menswear to the international market, today it is known for its Pitti peacocks, aka menswear street style, the likes of which have not been seen before, and the guest designers showcasing their collections during the four-day event.

Savile Row

This street in London's Mayfair, famous for its history of tailoring, is considered the capital of menswear. Home to brands Gieves & Hawkes, Huntsman, Norton & Sons, Welsh & Jefferies and Ozwald Boateng, among others, it is here that bespoke and made-to-measure suits come to life. It seems to be agreed that Henry Poole & Co was the first tailor to open on the street in 1846. The area had been built during the development of the Burlington Estate in the early 1700s and was named after the Earl of Burlington's wife, Lady Dorothy Savile. Tailors began to take premises in the 1800s. And it is here that military uniforms, as well as suits for the rich and famous, have since been – and continue to be – made.

Every house on Savile Row has a unique identity.
Patrick Grant, designer

Suit fashions

After World War II, working-class men began to adopt an Edwardian style of dress popularized by Savile Row tailors in the late 1940s. The Teddy Boys of the 1950s took this one step further with a look that involved a long, draped jacket, drainpipe trousers and creeper shoes – a subcultural take on tradition. In the United States, the zoot suit was another style of tailoring popular in the 1940s and 1950s, recognized for its wide shoulders, narrow waist and bright colours.

London Collections: Men

In 2012, London decided to introduce its own menswear fashion week, which was referred to as LCM, meaning 'London Collections: Men'. Up until this point, menswear offerings from London-based designers were shown the day after London Fashion Week ended, in a one-day showcase dedicated to menswear that was tacked on to the end. It is from this day, however, that the fashion world was introduced to Jonathan Anderson, who would go on to become the creative director of Loewe, as well as continue to run his own very successful brand.

In recent years Belgian Raf Simons and French-born Hedi Slimane have made significant contributions to menswear internationally – the former for his focus on youth-inspired collections and the latter during his tenures at both Dior Homme (2000–7), where he resurrected the fitted trouser, the dominant silhouette for the next 20 years, and Saint Laurent (2012–16).

The condensed idea
From flamboyance to function

04 Ready-to-Wear

Ready-to-wear is sometimes referred to as off-the-peg in the United Kingdom, or off-the-rack in the United States. In French, it translates as *prêt-à-porter* and is a manufacturing term that refers to clothes that are mass-produced by factories and available in a range of standard sizes.

In broad terms, ready-to-wear is what you will find when you go shopping on the high street, including to the designer stores, or when shopping online. A piece will not be unique or have been customized or tailored especially for you, unlike haute couture. In ready-to-wear, there are no fittings or appointments, and decisions are already made for you – which, in part, is why it became popular in the middle of the 20th century.

In 1798 the British writer Jane Austen wrote to a correspondent: 'I cannot determine what to do about my new Gown; I wish such things were to be bought ready-made.
Caroline Rennolds Milbank, *Icons of Fashion, The 20th Century*

The revealing of ready-to-wear collections forms the modern fashion calendar, in showcases that take place biannually, with womenswear shown in February/March, and then again in September/October. For menswear, events are held in January and June. The seasons are referred to as autumn/winter and spring/summer, shown six months before the collections will be available to buy in the stores. It is at these shows that most trends are born, or go viral. Though it used to be the case that the couture shows would wield their lavish influence on ready-to-wear, which in turn produced watered-down versions of garments and ideas, this is not so much the case nowadays.

Buyers, stylists, editors and journalists – the main groups that make up the fashion industry – attend the seasonal ready-to-wear collections and, after viewing the samples on the runway, will play a role in deciding which of them get put into production.

Evolution

Events that unfolded towards the end of the 19th century – the Industrial Revolution, economic growth and various technological advances in fashion, including sewing, cutting and embroidery – gave

Despite the elite and exclusive veneer of some luxury fashion houses, ready-to-wear is available for everyone, where couture is not, since a customer usually has to meet some sort of loyalty quota. Ready-to-wear can vary in price and quality due to the nature of the fashion house or brand, its history and prestige, and its target audience. Further offshoots of ready-to-wear can be seen in the rise of high street, or fast, fashion, which is a 21st-century development.

rise to the ready-to-wear phenomenon. Prior to this, and the emergence of haute couture before it, people typically made their own clothes, or employed the services of a seamstress or tailor. Sewing skills were expected of respectable women.

The concept of fashion – of wearing clothes for aesthetic reasons over utility – began to emerge during the 14th century, and changes in style can now be identified by centuries. Up until the 20th century, trends typically lasted for 100 years. After this, fashions tended to change by the decade, in part thanks to the advent of ready-to-wear, made possible by advancing technology.

In the years following World War II, women no longer wanted to spend time on lengthy couture fittings or pay the high prices that came with them, and especially for a design that might not be worn for a very long time. Work and social lives also no longer required the formality they once had; the 1960s especially would see the rise of a young and mobile generation, which coincided with a retail boom.

New York

While Paris had been busy establishing itself as the centre of couture and splendour, New York was doing the opposite and embracing mass manufacture, aided by the invention of the sewing machine, which evolved throughout the 1800s, and, later, the International Ladies' Garment Workers' Union, founded in 1900, which had ambitions to make New York the clothing capital of the world.

Seasonal ready-to-wear collections are shown at Fashion Weeks about six months ahead of when they will appear in the shops. This drives the fashion industry. The are four noted 'fashion capitals' – New York, London, Milan and Paris – and their fashion weeks follow on from one another in immediate succession as a centralized fashion body. This has not always been the case, as each city held its first fashion week in a different year.

- New York's first incarnation of New York Fashion Week, called 'press week' was in 1943. It was the brainchild of PR whizz Eleanor Lambert and took place at the Plaza Hotel.
- Though London established itself as a fashion hub during the 1960s, it was not until 1984 that the British Fashion Council debuted London Fashion Week.
- Milan instigated their fashion week in 1958, run by the then Camera Sindacale della Moda Italiana, now known as Camera Nazionale della Moda Italiana.
- Paris Fashion Week first took place in 1973, organized by the French Fédération.

The Garment District, located around Seventh Avenue, was already booming between 1828 and 1858, according to the Garment District Alliance. The introduction of the sewing machine resulted in a rapid fall in the price of clothing and therefore a rise in the scale of operations among the garment trade, which included the introduction of specialized machinery for lace-making and button-hole-making.

Records of ready-to-wear industry tabulated in the US Census of 1860 included hoop skirts, cloaks and mantillas.

Fairchild Dictionary of Fashion

Designers including Claire McCardell and Clare Potter had the objective to make women's clothes that were better suited to day-to-day living – more casual and less uptight. Following the success of Claire McCardell's Monastic dress, in particular, even Paris was now looking to New York to see what all the fuss was about and started to reconsider its snobbish attitude to ready-to-wear. Christian Dior-New York was launched in 1948 on the basis that there was a hunger for less expensive versions of haute couture designs. The brand would continue to expand under various shrewd uses of licensing agreement, such as perfume and nylon stockings.

In 1966, the famed French designer Yves Saint Laurent launched his own ready-to-wear brand called Rive Gauche. A chain of boutiques offered a separate, cheaper line of clothes, though made with just as much care; he would also offer a more affordable version of his iconic Le Smoking jacket. The first ready-to-wear Paris Fashion Week took place in 1973. The fashion industry was now working in a whole new way.

The condensed idea
Fashion for the masses

05 Sportswear

I n the 21st century, sportswear has morphed from being a separate type of clothing worn to perform a specific activity, to being an accepted form of day-to-day casualwear. Trainers can be – and are – worn with suits, and leggings are no longer just for yoga. In fact, many modern wardrobe staples are derived from sportswear garments. The polo shirt, made famous by René Lacoste, was initially intended for tennis (and before that polo) but is now a standard form of smart casual. As the world began to undo its top button to become less formal these past 150 years, the impact has been felt on our wardrobes.

The realms of high fashion have also been caught by the activewear bug, and ready-to-wear collections from designer houses have bounced around in taking inspiration from it. Notably, in 2014, both Chanel and Dior introduced highly decorated sneakers to their couture collections. And with the rise of street style and streetwear, sportswear has become a readily accepted part of the contemporary fashion wardrobe. In the early days of sport, almost the opposite was true with the latest fashions being worn for recreational activities.

Early developments

Back in the 1800s, it was impossible to take part in sports dressed in formal daywear, especially for women, who were restricted by corsets that made it difficult to breathe. The advent of the bicycle in the 1890s further contributed to entertaining the idea of divided skirts, or 'bloomers' (which had emerged in the 1850s), and a move towards more practical garments. Women would typically wear elements of men's clothes for sports, which were often made in heavy fabrications. The 1920s and 1930s brought a time of new freedom for women when it came to dressing for sport and leisure. Indeed, it was part of the wider opinion that it helped to promote health. And, at the same time, there was a string of designers ready with new ideas and more modern ways of dressing, such as Jean Patou and Coco Chanel.

Tennis

First played in France, in the Middle Ages, the game was introduced to the United States in 1874, where it was known as lawn tennis. At the time, corresponding attire would reflect the current fashions – for women, perhaps, a bustle or a bulbous leg-of-mutton sleeve. Men wore long flannel trousers with white shirts (it has been traditional for players to wear white). It would not be until sometime later that the French fashion designer Jean Patou introduced the tennis skirt, thought to be first worn by French tennis player Suzanne Lenglen at Wimbledon, in 1921.

Owing to a shift in silhouette, sportier styles became popular from the 1920s, where straight lines and function became symbols of modernity and left behind the cloying and claustrophobic styles of the past. American tennis player Gussie Moran introduced short dresses with ruffle knickers in the 1940s, and mini-skirts and microskirt dresses appeared in the 1960s.

Patou also created clothes for modern women who wanted to give the impression they were active. Lenglen would wear calf-length pleated skirts and sleeveless cardigans. Simplicity was key. Patou was also among those who popularized and promoted bathing suits, which, like outfits for tennis – as well as golf, bicycling, ice-skating, yachting and hunting – are among the earliest forms of sportswear.

Stretch

Of significance to the evolution of sportswear has been innovation in fabrics, especially those that are stretchy. Materials with stretch have a long history, with knitted and woven textiles known as far back as ancient Egyptian times – the Victoria and Albert Museum, in London, has a pair of socks dated between the 3rd and 5th century CE in its collection. Knitted headwear has been known since the 15th century and English Queen Elizabeth I was apparently presented with a pair of knitted silk hose in the 16th century. There have been versions of knitted or elastic gilets, trousers and corsets, and early bathing suits were made from wool before an elasticized one-piece took over.

Jersey, a soft and stretchy knitted fabric, has its roots in the Channel Island of Jersey, where it was first used to make knitted garments. By the end of the 19th century, it had made the jump into sportswear and was worn by athletes. The fabric would be popular with a new wave of designers who proffered comfort and ease of movement. The development of new fabrics during the first half of the 20th century – a boom time in the evolution of sportswear – would pave the way for a

Known for many things, including quilted handbags, the little black dress and No.5 perfume, Coco Chanel is also synonymous with bringing a sporting sensibility to clothing. The designer's general philosophy was that leisure clothes made the foundations for modern fashionable dressing. They were comfortable and chic. Many of her designs were adapted from menswear and it was she who introduced yachting pants, as she called them, based on a sailor's trouser, for women. These were followed by beach pyjamas, which proffered an overall gamine look.

whole new way of dressing. By the 1950s, there was nylon, and in 1958 Lycra. Gore-Tex, first used in the 1970s, enables breathability as well as being waterproof.

The United States leads the way

Just as the French have become associated with haute couture, the Americans are synonymous with sportswear, and it is widely thought that this is their unique contribution to the history of fashion, or costume. At the same time that Paris was becoming a hub for detail, craft and exclusivity, the United States was modernizing and catering to the new boom in ready-to-wear, which by its very nature was geared towards an active life.

With a career that began in earnest during the 1930s, Claire McCardell studied at Parsons School of Design in New York and became known as the creator of American sportswear. Along with her contemporaries, she established the city's Seventh Avenue as the centre of US fashion. McCardell favoured simple and direct designs, creating non-traditional garments that were free-flowing and without structural or confining elements. Hers were city clothes that were all about comfort in an age of formality. Among her best-known designs are the Monastic dress (1938), which was loose-fitting and belted at the waist; the Pop-over dress (1942) and diaper bathing suits (1944).

Tracksuits started off as two-piece outfits worn by athletes (on the track), not by the public. It was in the 1970s that they started to make the transition as exercise wear became fashionable. It was around this time that American designer, Norma Kamali, was making sportswear fashionable with her sweatshirt and legging creations.

In 1985, American fashion designer Donna Karan introduced her famous Seven Easy Pieces, drawing on body-conscious forms to create sportswear-infused looks for the office. This translated as stretchy and supple fabrics that built on the pared-back and forward-thinking nature of Claire McCardell's designs back in the 1930s and 1940s. Multipurpose clothing was key and Karan developed 'the body', which was a leotard-like piece with snappers.

To this day, America is known for its preppy and smart-casual styles, such as those by Ralph Lauren, which are imbued with early sportswear references and a kind of Ivy League prestige, and sportswear giants Nike. Recognized by its swoosh logo, and plethora of prestigious and global ambassadors, the brand has a history tracking back to 1962.

Athleisure

In recent years, a new genre of sportswear has come to light, 'athleisure', which combines athletics and leisure wear. The idea here is that garments are designed to look like you can exercise in them rather than actually being worn to exercise in (though in some you can do that too). Brands auch as Sweaty Betty and Lululemon would be considered athleisure, promoting a casual loungewear feel that became popular during the Covid-19 pandemic.

The condensed idea
A largely American fashion revolution

06 Leather

Making leather, one of the core materials used for the crafting of our shoes, bags, wallets, belts and other fashion accessories, as well as garments such as the iconic leather jacket, is an ancient practice with a history of more than 7,000 years. Since primitive times, leather has been used to make shoes and clothing, and many other useful things, including saddles, book covers and footballs.

Leather has several advantageous properties: it is durable, strong, flexible and malleable. It is also water-resistant and can withstand extreme wear and tear, which is why it has always been a popular choice for equestrian accessories and shoes, from sandals to boots, over the centuries.

The process of making leather started with animal skins being dried in the sun, softened using animal fats and preserved through salting and smoking. The Egyptians and Hebrews developed the process of vegetable tanning, the treatment that makes it leather, around 400 BCE. They did so using resources such as tree bark. Leather tanning was widespread in Europe by the 15th century, with various processes industrialized by the mid-19th century.

Modern-day and commercial leather-making involves the preparation of the hide for tanning, the tanning itself and then the processing of the tanned leather. Vegetable tanning is the oldest of the tanning methods and can take weeks or months to complete. The end result is a resistant and solid leather. Other methods include mineral tanning and oil tanning. Once hides have been tanned, they are dyed, with oils and greases applied before the leather is dried. It is then stretched and softened and ready to be turned into the item for which it is intended. Sueding and shearling are examples of finishes.

The leather jacket

In fashion, there is one particular item – beyond shoes and bags – for which leather is known and that is the leather jacket. It is alluring, cool, macho, intimidating, sexy and solid. Among the best-known styles is the Schott Perfecto 'lancer style', a motorcycle jacket worn by Marlon Brando in *The Wild One* (1953), designed by Irving Schott in 1928. It was intended specifically for the motorcycle market and early

Hide

When talking about leather, the word 'hide' is often used. This refers to the skin of the animal. Hide is typically used to refer to that of a larger animal, while 'skin' is used to refer to that of smaller animals. It is the skin or hide that is tanned – a process that preserves it so that it can become a sturdy and functional material. Leathers mostly come from cattle, sheep and lambs, goats and kids, equine animals, buffalo, pigs and aquatic animals such as seals, whales and alligators. But skins of other animals have been used. In recent years, the animal rights organization People for the Ethical Treatment of Animals (PETA) has focused on campaigning against fashion's use of leather, having made successful inroads with banning fur.

versions were made from horsehide, which is known for its durability and being hard to wear in (as leather jackets often notoriously are).

The leather jacket also plays a significant role in the film *Grease* (1978) and John Travolta's smooth, suave character Danny, a stud. Olivia Newton-John, who played Sandy, was famously sewn into her leather-look trousers for the final dance scene because the zip broke. Her character's transformation from naive and innocent is signalled by her lean look, complete with leather jacket.

Happy Days' Fonzie wears a leather jacket to show he is edgier than his 1950s preppy high-school counterparts. Here, a sign of rebellion, danger – no doubt in part because its intended use was for protection on a motorcycle – the outsider, the outcast, the hero. *Indiana Jones*, *Easy Rider*, *Top Gun* and *Mad Max* are all films in which the protagonist wears a leather jacket. Such characters typically prompt a swoon, giving the garment sex appeal.

Further examples of onscreen leather-wearing include Arnold Schwarzenegger's black biker in *The Terminator* franchise, Brad Pitt's red leather style as Tyler Durden in *Fight Club* and the multitude of leather jackets, coats and jumpsuits in the *Matrix*. All of them convey otherworldliness, the outsider, or outlier.

Craft makers

French fashion designer Claude Montana is best known for using leather to create strong silhouettes, such as broad-shouldered coats and jackets, during the 1970s. His designs had a toughness and almost aggression to them. And while many luxury fashion houses use leather in their offering, there are a handful that have built their reputations specifically on leather craft. These include French Hermès, Spanish Loewe and Italian Gucci.

Hermès dates back to 1837 when it was a saddler or harness maker. Thierry Hermès opened a workshop in rue Basse-du-Rempart in Paris. It is well known for producing handcrafted leather goods, particularly bags such as the Kelly and the Birkin, named after actresses Grace Kelly and Jane Birkin, respectively.

Loewe began life in 1846 as a collective of leather artisans based in Spain. The brand itself is named after a German craftsman, Enrique Loewe, who joined the collective in 1872 and has been credited with unifying it. It began producing ready-to-wear in the 1960s and was acquired by the luxury goods conglomerate LVMH in 1996. Following a series of creative director appointments, Jonathan Anderson was given the top job in 2013 and has been making waves there ever since.

Gucci, meanwhile, was founded by Guccio Gucci in Florence, Italy, in 1921, and started as a leather goods and luggage retailer. The business stayed in the family and was taken on by his sons and grandson, Maurizio Gucci. They took traditional accessories and gave them an equestrian spin. Bags and shoes followed, with ready-to-wear debuting in the 1960s. Today Gucci is part of the French luxury group Kering, and known more for its eclectic sense of design, thanks to Italian Alessandro Michele, who was creative director from 2015–22, and for sexiness from 1994–2004 via American Tom Ford. Frida Giannini was creative director for a time from 2006; and Sabato De Sarno joined the house in 2023.

Leather alternatives

Some of the earliest leather substitutes were invented in the 19th century. Nitrocellulose, or guncotton, developed by German chemist Friedrich Schönbein in 1845, was turned into collodion, or pyroxylin in 1846, by French artist Louis-Nicolas Ménard. The latter was used as a protective coating in wound dressings and later applied to materials.

The American DuPont Fabrikoid company patented Fabrikoid in 1915, having developed it in 1910 – a pyroxylin-infused cotton fabric. Because it resisted water, it was used for items such as upholstery, linings and car covers.

A brand of synthetic leather called naugahyde, fabric coated with leather fibres and rubber, was first used in women's handbags in the early 1920s. Since the 1960s, fabrics have been coated in, or infused with, polyurethane and polyvinyl chloride, which give the look and durability of leather.

Faux, or imitation, leather and pleather has a similar appearance and strength to leather at a lower cost and is ethically considerate to animals, though environmentalists have criticized the amount of plastic used in artificial and faux leathers, which makes them non-reusable and they cannot be recycled later. More recently, there has been an explosion in the plant-based leather industry.

Alternatives have included mushroom and pineapple. Stella McCartney, the fashion designer known for her eco and ethical credentials (when she launched the brand some 20 years ago, she set out to be the first luxury house not to use leather, feathers, fur or skins), introduced two garments – not for sale – made from vegan, lab-grown Mylo™ mushroom leather. It was innovated by the brand's long-term partner Bolt Threads and is made from mycelium, which is a root-like structure of fungi. It is also not petroleum-based, which a lot of synthetic alternatives can be.

The condensed idea
Reliable and strong, but where next?

07 Fastenings

How did you get dressed today? Zipping up a pair of trousers, buttoning up a shirt? In clothing, fastenings are the devices that enable a garment to be put on and taken off with ease – and, pointedly, by the wearer themselves. Even up until the 20th century, it was common practice for women – especially among wealthier classes – to have help when getting dressed. A corset, for example, required someone else to lace it and tighten it from the back.

Feats of technological ingenuity, fastenings have enabled clothing to evolve and, in many ways, take up less space in our lives. They are symbols of modernity, promoting the correct fit and creating shape and silhouette. They have streamlined our lifestyles and our fashion styles, fulfilling both aesthetic and functional roles. Buttons, hooks-and-eyes, zips and Velcro may be small details of design but they have had a huge impact.

Buttons

Available in many shapes and sizes, materials and finishes, buttons are the disc-like pieces of solid material with holes in the middle that slide through a piece of fabric to fasten it through a corresponding buttonhole. It is thought that buttons and buttonholes emerged in the

Special designs

In the mid-18th century, English manufacturer Matthew Boulton debuted a cut-steel button that was made by attaching polished steel facets to a steel blank. Designed to catch the light and sparkle, they were very popular among gentlemen at the time, but they were also very expensive. Boulton apparently had books of designs for customers to choose from. He is one of the best-known makers of cut-steel jewellery. At the beginning of the 19th century, a less-expensive version was introduced and gilded brass buttons became popular.

13th or 14th centuries. Before they came along, garments were laced together or fastened with brooches and clasps. Buttons could be used to indicate wealth or rank – made of gold, silver and ivory, for example. Those made from bone or wood were more common, however, sometimes used as a base to then cover with fabric. In the 18th century pewter was used to make stamped-out buttons. Calamine brass buttons were also in use, as were embroidered buttons.

Ceramic, glass, porcelain, metal, animal horn and lacquer have all been used at various times by different cultures. The French, for example, decorated porcelain buttons by hand using paint; the Czech Republic, historically known as Bohemia, produced coloured glass versions; and in Japan, ceramic buttons were hand-painted with traditional motifs. Lacquered papier-mache buttons became popular in Europe in the late 1800s. In the United States, in the 1890s, American manufacturer John F Boepple started to use mussel shells found along the Mississippi River, where before only seashell had been used.

By the 20th century, buttons became less decorative and more utilitarian. Often, they were also eclipsed by the debut of the zipper, which was less fiddly and faster. Increasingly, they would now be made from plastic and mass-production meant machines could make moulded buttons. This, in turn, has led to the value of old buttons increasing – many are collector's items today, noted for their workmanship, rarity and artwork.

Hook-and-eye fastening

Just like the button, the hook-and-eye closure has been almost entirely usurped by the zip in contemporary clothing. Featuring a small metal hook on one side and either an embroidered loop or small metal loop on the opposite side, the fastening was used for shirtwaists (a woman's blouse that looks like a shirt) and dresses in the late 19th and early 20th centuries.

Zips

The zip, or a slide fastener as it was exhibited by Whitcomb L Judson at the World's Columbian Exposition in Chicago, 1893, was first called a clasp locker and saw a series of hooks and eyes with a side clasp for closing and opening. It was a Swedish engineer named Gideon

Zipped

While Whitcomb L Judson's name might be more readily associated with the zip and its origins, a similar device had been patented by Elias Howe – who also invented a sewing machine – in 1851. But it was not deemed to be any vast improvement on the hook-and-eye or the button. Howe's Automatic, Continuous Clothing Closure was hard to use and rusted easily. It also snagged and was expensive. It did not catch on.

Sundback who switched out the hooks and eyes for spring clips and created the Hookless #2. Considered the first modern zip, it went on sale in 1914 and was granted a patent three years later. In 1911, a similar kind of device had been patented in Europe by Katharina Kuhn-Moos and Henri Forster but was said never to have been manufactured. In 1917, the US Navy had equipped windproof flying suits with slide fasteners. B G Work, of the B F Goodrich Company, is said to have given the device the name 'zipper' in 1923.

After its invention, the zip did not enter fashion realms until the 1930s, when it was widely used for handbags and trousers. It soon gained a reputation for being rebellious, sexy even, featuring as it did on the leather jacket. It would be reinvented several times thereafter – for example, with the introduction of new materials such as nylon during the 1960s. Sometimes a zip is a visible part of a design in a bright colour and other times is concealed to give a sleek silhouette. Where buttons and hooks-and-eyes took time to fasten, were fiddly, and felt old-fashioned, zips were slick, fast and felt futuristic, – as long as they didn't jam. Today, the zip remains ever prevalent in everything from bags and boots to coats and trousers, skirts and performance wear.

Velcro

Faster still, instant even, is Velcro – its name taken from the trademark for a nylon pile fabric that fastens to itself via tiny loops on a strip of woolly fabric, which snag onto hooks on a corresponding strip of the same material. It is most often used in performance wear, sportswear and childrenswear, as well as trainers. It is useful for stage costumes that require quick changes.

The Swiss engineer George de Mestral invented it in the 1940s. He had noticed that a plant called cockle-bur stuck to his socks and the fur of his dog while they walked in the woods. The new type of fastener was patented in the mid-1950s by Velcro SA.

Of all the fastenings, Velcro is the least likely to be found in high fashion unless a collection is expressly linked to the outdoors and performance. Likewise, it is unlikely to be found in high-street offerings. But is sometimes used to fasten a bag internally, or as straps on trainers. It has a characteristic scratching sound when it is opened, the loudest of all the listed fastenings.

The condensed idea
Small details, huge technological implications

08 Knitwear

The exact origins of knitting are unclear, but the craft of hand-knitting has been practised in different parts of the world over many centuries; it can be traced back to the ancient Egyptians, for example. Knitting is the act of interlocking one loop of yarn through another, using two needles, to create fabric. It can be done by hand or machine (the latter since the 19th century) and has played an important role in creating freedom and comfort in clothing for the wearer, especially in sportswear, because it adds greater elasticity to the fabric than weaving.

According to London's Victoria and Albert Museum, archaeological finds in medieval cities show that the use of knitted goods in Europe spread from the 14th century and knitting guilds are thought to have developed around this time. Knitted stockings were apparently introduced to Queen Elizabeth I around 1530. In England, such a thing as The Cappers Act of 1571 said that everyone over the age of six years, with various exceptions depending on class and status, should wear a wool-knit cap on Sundays and holidays (except when travelling). This kept their makers steadily employed. Knitting was in common use for underwear during the late 1800s.

'Knitwear' first came into use during the 1920s and 1930s. Manufacturers had previously used the term 'hosiery' to define all aspects of knitted garments, from vests to combinations to swimwear. But the new term would now come to mean outerwear as well as underwear. A knitted coat department had been formed by the Scottish knitwear manufacturer Pringle of Scotland in 1910. The fashion author Marnie Fogg has noted that, as knitwear moved into outerwear items, garments were not dictated by the engineering skills of the framework knitter – the person who operates the treadles – but by the design process. Among the benefits of knitwear was its versatility, which meant it could fit a variety of body types and was especially suitable for outdoor sporting activities.

Sweaters became popular in the 1920s (the economic depression that followed the Wall Street Crash saw a return to hand-knitting), and by the 1950s new and more flexible fibres were blended with wool to create a broader range of designs and colours.

William Lee, from Nottingham, invented the stocking frame, which was the first mechanical knitting machine, in 1589. It gently took over from the hand-knitting industry as developments in technology enabled it to become more refined and efficient. Fast forward almost another half century and the introduction of Lastex, in 1925, meant further innovation. This is the US Rubber Company's trade name for an elastic yarn that is made from rubber combined with silk, cotton or rayon. It was used particularly in underwear or foundation garments such as girdles and corsets in the early part of the 20th century. Because it was elasticized, it therefore enabled the fabric to retain its shape better, and started to become used in swimwear collections.

With the 1960s and 1970s came a revival for home-knitting. Paco Rabanne's famous space-age-infused designs saw chain links added to knitwear, proving the technique could be just as futuristic as it could be homespun and domestic. It was during the 1970s that knitwear received some high-fashion kudos as it became a key component of the ready-to-wear market. And, accordingly, knitwear designers offered top-to-toe looks rather than just accessories.

Prominent designers

Surrealist fashion designer Elsa Schiaparelli's career began with her trompe l'oeil knitwear. But there are other designers whose creations had a significant impact on the evolution and perception of the technique, which has ultimately been able to modernize the ready-to-wear industry and, when done by hand, rarify the world of couture.

Husband-and-wife design team Ottavio Missoni and Rosita Jelmini founded the knitwear brand Missoni in 1953. Ottavio had previously owned a firm that made tracksuits and Rosita had worked for her family's bedding company. They began the business with a few knitting machines and started to produce knitwear that they sold to

The twinset

The twinset – a matching sweater and a cardigan of the same colour, and typically featuring a round neck – is a fashion classic associated with knitwear. Various different styles have been introduced over the years. It is associated with two British manufacturers in particular: John Smedley and Pringle of Scotland. Pringle of Scotland hired its first dedicated knitwear designer, Otto Weisz, in 1934. In 1947, it was reportedly the best-selling brand in the United States. It was known for its intarsia design, also known as argyle, which was popular on the golf course. The two-piece, frequently worn with a string of pearls, has come to move away from its original sporting roots, and is often thought of as prim and proper.

other designers. By the 1970s, they were manufacturing under their own label and producing highly individual knitwear pieces in striking patterns and designs that blended colour in exciting ways. They later expanded their designs to home furnishings.

Missoni offered the international customer an entire wardrobe from knit and did a huge amount to alter fashion's attitude towards it. Their first boutique opened in Milan in 1976, followed by Paris, Japan and New York. In 1997, their daughter Angela took over the creative directorship of the house. The brand is as synonymous with its chevrons and knits today as it ever was.

In Paris, there was Sonia Rykiel. The designer opened her first boutique in 1968 on Paris's Left Bank, which at the time was associated with bohemian style and therefore helped throw off any frumpy connotations knitwear might have had. Rykiel elevated knitwear, making it contemporary and cool, sexy and lithe. She was known, in particular, for her stripes, and

> No one knows how to knit like the Italians, and Missoni knitwear is definitely finely tuned, with a background of supreme technology.
>
> Linda Watson, *Vogue Fashion*

also incorporated text and decoration into her knits. During the 1960s, she was dubbed the 'queen of knitwear'.

Tunisian designer Azzedine Alaïa moved knit away from the casual connotations it held, and into the rarified world of high fashion and luxury. Experimenting with yarns, tension, cutouts and body-hugging silhouettes, Alaïa created an innovative, sexier knitwear aesthetic that would be championed by the next generation of knitwear designers, among them Louise Goldin, Mark Fast and Craig Lawrence. Louise Goldin has been hailed a genius in knitwear for her fusion of technology with wearable design, while Mark Fast championed plus-size models on the catwalk early on with his part-bright neon knits.

The condensed idea
Clothing designed with comfort in mind

09 The Sewing Machine

I n 1860, *The New York Times* declared, in an article dated 7 January, that America had delivered many technical feats to the world and the sewing machine, patented in 1846, was one of them. The first widely distributed home appliance, the sewing machine was a great technological advance for fashion and the clothing industry. Fabric could now be stitched together mechanically using a needle powered by treadle, or electricity. Speeding up the whole garment-making process, this led to the evolution of ready-to-wear.

The New York Times article points out that it was one of the most important labour-saving inventions, and that, notably, its invention was of most benefit to women – an ability to sew was deemed more or less a requirement of women (or certainly 'respectable' women), until the middle of the 20th century. The machines most in use at the time for manufacturing purposes, it claimed, were those made by I M Singer & Co and Wheeler & Wilson; adoption for general use then seems to have been faster than for any other invention.

Innovation

There are many inventions without which it is hard to imagine getting by today and the sewing machine is undoubtedly one of them. British fashion academic Elizabeth Wilson acknowledges that, without it, the mass fashion industry could not have come into being.

Prior to its arrival, which is largely pegged to an early sewing machine designed and manufactured by Barthélemy Thimonnier of France (though there do seem to have been various designs in

Fashion City
The 2024 exhibition, Fashion City, How Jewish Londoners Shaped Global Style (at London's Museum of Docklands), detailed how a sewing machine was advised as being the most important tool for newcomers setting up as tailors in 1905. Further, they could be rented from charitable networks of the Jewish Board of Guardians if money was tight.

Mass production and the growth of factories did not prevent the existence of sweatshops, which were already common. Much work was carried out in appalling conditions throughout the late-18th and early-19th centuries. Hours were long and there were no regulations in force.

development prior to this), clothes were made by hand, mostly by women or by professionals who offered services such as tailoring. In 1830, Thimonnier obtained a contract from the French government to mass-produce uniforms for the French army. But, fearing the invention would ruin their livelihoods, about 200 tailors rioted and destroyed the machines in 1831. They would not be the only ones who had concerns.

Next came Walter Hunt, from New York City, who is credited with improving the machine's design around 1832–34, though it was apparently never patented, and then Elias Howe, from Spencer, Massachusetts, whose machine was patented in 1846. Common to both machines was a curved, eye-pointed needle that moved in an arc as it carried thread through the fabric and, on the other side, interlocked with a second thread that was carried by a shuttle running back and forth.

Howe's design was both successful and widely copied to the extent it became part of a patent pool – where companies agree to cross-licence products relating to a certain type of technology – which included the design of Isaac Singer, whose name is probably more commonly associated with the machine today.

Isaac Singer

Born on 27 October 1811, in Pittstown, New York, Isaac Merritt Singer was an American inventor credited with developing and bringing into general use the first practical domestic sewing machine. He became an apprentice machinist aged 19 and, by 1839, had already patented a rock-drilling machine. Singer further patented a metal-and-wood-carving machine 10 years later.

Sewing statistics

In 1860, reportedly more than 110,000 sewing machines were produced in the United States alone. Over time, the design of the modern sewing machine evolved to become specialized for industrial purposes but the very basic and pragmatic purpose of it has remained unchanged.

The introduction of half a million sewing machines worldwide in 1871, compared to just over 2,000 in 1853, contributed to a fall in the price of clothing and therefore the scale of production could increase. Items such as hosiery and underwear were the first to be constructed entirely by machine. Functions such as simple seaming could speed up 30 fold through automation and the production of garments increased by 500 per cent. The sewing machine paved the way for further mechanization in the fields of buttonholing, lace-making and embroidery, which meant further goods were able to benefit from these techniques.

It was while working in a machine shop in Boston in 1851 that Singer was asked to repair a sewing machine. The model in question was by Lerow & Blodgett. Within just 11 days, he had come to design and build an improved model, which he patented and sold through I M Singer & Company.

A particular feature of Singer's machine was an overhanging arm that held the needle bar over a horizontal table, so making it possible to sew any part of the work and to allow continuous and curved stitching. His machine also featured the basic eye-pointed needle and the lock stitch, which had been a development of Elias Howe. This led to Howe winning a patent-infringement suit against him in 1854, but Singer persevered with his machines. In 1851, he formed a partnership with businessman Edward Clark, and by 1860 their company had become the largest producer of sewing machines in the world.

Singer won first prize at the Exposition Universelle in Paris, in 1855, and would go on to show the first workable electric sewing machine in 1885 at the Philadelphia electric exhibition. The mass-production of domestic electric machines began in 1910. Singer is also credited with being ahead of the times when it came to marketing, and promoted the use of instalment payment plans. He would obtain a further 12 patents to cover improvements to his machine. In 1863, he and Clark formed the Singer Manufacturing Company; in 1963 it became the Singer Company.

Divisions

While it had its benefits, the sewing machine created a divide between traditional craft workers, who made everything by hand, and semi-skilled machinists. Tailors had been among the first independent craftspeople and up until the 17th century, customers who wanted their clothes commercially made bought the cloth and took it to them. Now, working in parallel, there was demand for the fine needlework that could only be done by hand and mass production. Between 1890 and 1910, the mass-produced clothing industry really took off in the United Kingdom and the United States. Along with France, they were among the first to use factories to make clothes for their armed forces.

While it would go on to democratize fashion for the consumer and be efficient for a new and industrialized world, mechanization put the jobs of skilled craftspeople at risk. At the same time, it would also make what they did even more special and prestigious. In the 21st century, hand-crafted work, such as the type seen in modern haute couture, is widely celebrated.

The condensed idea
Speeding up production

10 Denim

Today, denim is ubiquitous in our wardrobes, a daily staple, worn for both smart and casual occasions and available in a multitude of designs, techniques, finishes, dyes and washes. As a fabric, it is most synonymous with jeans, which have played a significant role in the history of denim and its popularity (the two are almost interchangeable).

Due to its durability, denim started out life as workwear. It is linked especially with Levis Strauss. Though he is only part of the story. In 1853, amid the gold rush, Levis Strauss opened a branch of the family business in California – not trading in denim or jeans yet, but dried goods. Several years later, during the 1870s, a Nevada tailor named Jacob Davis started producing hard-wearing work trousers, made using a cotton fabric, for his labourer and miner clientele. He is thought to have approached Levi Strauss for financial backing and, according to the Levi's brand, the pair combined copper rivet reinforcements, which prevented rips, with the tough denim, leading to the manufacture of waist overalls in 1873, or what are now called blue jeans.

> By the 20th century, 'jean' was the term for a wide range of cotton or denim informal trousers.
>
> *Vogue France*

Such was the demand for the overalls that Strauss opened a factory in San Francisco. The trademark leather patch was added to the rear of the waistband in the 1880s, and from the 1890s the company began to produce a version of the popular Levi's 501 style. Levi's was one of the top three best-known US manufacturers of denim workwear in the 20th century, the other two being H D Lee Mercantile Company (later, Lee) and the Blue Bell Overall Company (later, Wrangler). H D Lee Company had been producing a hardwearing denim twill for its workwear ranges since 1952.

Work and play

Jeans went from being workwear to leisurewear with style status, thanks to Hollywood. The studios at the time, circa 1930, were producing a lot of Westerns and their stars would often wear denim.

It was all about the myth of the cowboy. Cowboys, of course, did wear jeans because they were hardwearing. They also happened to look cool. Such was the popularity of Westerns that the United States opened vacation spots called 'dude ranches', which brought to life the whole cowboy experience, and this meant dressing the part in denim. They were incredibly popular from the 1930s through to the 1950s.

On screen, jeans started to symbolize rebellion, youth and sex appeal in much the same way that leather had done. In *Rebel Without a Cause* (1955), a film about the moral decay of American youth, James Dean and his youthful crew of teenagers all wore jeans. The star, Elvis Presley, thought of as obscene for his dance moves at the time, wore them, too, in *Loving You* and *Jailhouse Rock*, both 1957. The American heartthrob would only have cemented their risqué style status.

Through the decades

Jeans, during the 1970s, went tight and flared. In the 1980s, stone-washed jeans with high waists were popular – now described as 'mom' jeans. But it is through the 1990s and into the 2000s that jeans have

De Nîmes

The name 'denim' comes from the French town Nîmes. It is a cotton twill weave fabric of white and blue threads that was used as workwear in the 20th century because it was strong, durable and washable. It was particularly popular in the 1970s, and then again in the 1990s, having first been made into dresses, skirts and jackets by the 1940s. Its most famous export, of course, is as trousers, or jeans.

The word 'jeans' is thought to come from Genes, French for Genoa, Italy, a port where sailors apparently wore sturdy work trousers. After jeans, denim jackets – also known as jean jackets – are probably the best-known item made from the enduring fabric. Denim and jeans have largely become an emblem associated with youth culture.

Canadian tuxedo

The term 'Canadian tuxedo' refers to wearing double denim, a pair of jeans with a denim jacket. Popstars Britney Spears and Justin Timberlake famously wore denim, he in the Canadian tuxedo, she in a denim ballgown, for the 2001 American Music Awards. The double denim look was once frowned upon but has now become a readily accepted and stylish combination, adopted by a host of celebrities. The term is thought to have originated from a time in 1951 when Bing Crosby was refused entry to a hotel in Vancouver because he was wearing jeans and a denim jacket or shirt.

seen their heyday, with practically every subculture being identified by their denim choice. Styles include everything from baggy (JNCO) to decorated (True Religion, Von Dutch, Ed Hardy), distressed (Dolce & Gabbana, DSquared2), hip-hop streetwear (FUBU) to designer and premium (A.P.C., Acne Studios). Premium Japanese raw denim brands such as Evisu became extremely popular too, even more exclusive for a time than designer denim, the notion of which had been introduced by Calvin Klein.

Designer denim

Calvin Klein made jeans famous in 1980 with a series of adverts featuring Brooke Shields, which caused controversy because of the undertones of underage sexuality. Shields was only 15 at the time, provocatively posed and accompanied by suggestive straplines. The campaign caused outrage – and sold two million pairs of jeans in a month.

In contrast, denim has also become a specialized craft for some designers who have used it as a signature. In the early 2010s, French designer Faustine Steinmetz explored couture techniques using denim, while Portuguese duo Marta Marques and Paulo Almeida of Marques Almeida made the unravelling and frayed edges a motif of their real and authentic designs.

Today, it is widely accepted to wear denim in most situations: to work, providing it is smart, and to some restaurants, providing there are no rips. About the only places where it is still considered taboo are private members clubs and some venues in prestige hotels.

Interestingly, in 2022 and 2023, a trend emerged for non-denim denim, where various fashion houses, including Bottega Veneta and Balenciaga, featured pieces in their collections that were made to look like denim but were in fact made of leather or canvas, respectively.

The condensed idea
Cool classic with hardwearing roots

11 Bias Cut

French designer Madeleine Vionnet, who popularized the cowl neckline and the halterneck, is widely acknowledged as being a pioneer of the bias cut, a technique that emerged circa 1923. It was around this time that there was a shift in the structure of clothes from straight, almost tubular, to more body conscious, and Vionnet was experimenting in this area. The technique, which is fairly complicated, involves cutting across the grain, rather than along it, and results in an elegant and streamlined silhouette. It was a revelation that propelled Vionnet to the height of fame.

Madeleine Vionnet

Born in 1876, in Aubervilliers, France, Madeleine Vionnet apprenticed as a dressmaker aged 11 or 12, where she learned the process of making lingerie. She then built upon her skills as a seamstress with a London court dressmaker. She returned to Paris circa 1900, to work for the design house Callot Soeurs, and in 1907, joined the French fashion house Doucet. She opened her own house in 1912, which closed for a short spell during World War I.

What makes Vionnet significant is a technical contribution to fashion that many say is unrivalled. One of several anti-corset designers who emerged around the 1880s, she rejected traditional dressmaking, instead fitting pieces together directly on the body or mannequin, draping, pinning and cutting the cloth to the form, in order to create her fluid lines.

Technicality

Fabric has a warp and a weft – horizontal and vertical lines that cross at right angles to form a straight grain. Vionnet is thought to have cut her fabric on the straight of the grain, but then turned the pattern pieces so they draped on the bias.

In ancient Rome and Greece, cloth was highly prized and therefore considered too special to cut. Instead it was fashioned through folding, wrapping, pinning and gathering around the body.

- The ancient Greek *chiton* was a tunic made from a rectangle of cloth that was folded over the body and held using clasps.
- The ancient Greek *peplos* was a rectangle of cloth that hung from the shoulders and was then belted around the waist.
- The *toga*, a garment worn by male Roman citizens and noted for its draped appearance, comes from ancient Etruscan culture and was supposedly based on a long, wrapped garment called a *tebenna*. Owing to its impracticality, the toga was worn by those who led a wealthy and leisurely lifestyle.

The bias cut was already known in the making of collars and sleeves but Vionnet introduced it to dressmaking, drawing on her lingerie background to add panels that wrapped around the body instead of requiring the traditional darts or unsightly fastenings. She used the fabric in a clever way to achieve seamless drapery, often using wider fabric than was usual to accommodate her draping, resulting in flowing but form-fitting silhouettes. She was inspired by classical antiquity, experimenting with the chiton and peplos forms of ancient Greece.

After Vionnet

Vionnet retired in 1939, but other designers had also been experimenting with draping techniques. Spanish designer Mariano Fortuny is known for the Delphos dress, which was in part inspired by the Ionian chiton, a type of unisex tunic worn in ancient Greece. Fortuny's dress is thought to have appeared as early as 1907 and was patented in 1909. It had a statuesque quality about it and featured a special pleating process which, to this day, designers remain baffled as to how exactly it was executed, such was the technicality of its creation. Fortuny made finely pleated garments that, it is thought, required almost four times the average width of material.

Just after Vionnet, American designer Elizabeth Hawes was also experimenting with cut. Her Diamond Horseshoe dress, which debuted in 1936, is her best-known design. It shows off the back – sunbathing had become a popular pastime – and skims the body. The bodice is formed from a single piece of fabric that has been gently gathered, while seaming at the back shows off a streamlined silhouette.

In the modern world, from the 18th century onwards, a number of neoclassical movements in fashion have drawn on the soft, draped styles of the classical past.
Fashion: The Ultimate Book of Costume and Style

In the early 1930s, the French designer Madame Grès opened up her shop, La Maison Alix, in Paris (known as Grès from 1939). She draped her jersey designs directly onto the body with the aim of keeping the number of seams to a minimum. Her designs, also a little like ancient Greek robes, used gathers to create cascading falls that prevented the exposure of any flesh. What seemed simple at a glance in fact boasted great detail. A noted master of draping, Grès often used asymmetric shapes.

There is also Jean Dessès, a Greek designer known for his chiffon and silk muslin dresses, closely draped onto the body in soft powdery colours. He opened his own couture maison in 1937. It was not long after this that Claire McCardell – known for her role in the rise of American ready-to-wear – joined this cohort of designers with her Monastic dress design, which was bias cut and tied at the waist with a rope.

Hollywood

It was American costume designer Gilbert Adrian who, in 1933, introduced Parisian couture to the United States mass market, with his bias-cut backless dress for Jean Harlow. Known as the Goddess gown, it featured in the film *Dinner at Eight*.

For John Galliano, who rose to fashion fame during the 1990s and has worked for Dior and Maison Margiela, bias cut is one of his signature styles. In 2011, he created a custom bias-cut wedding dress for the model Kate Moss that took its style cues from *The Great Gatsby*. Sophia Kokosalaki, the late Greek designer based in London in the 2000s, was also well known for her use of drape. Vionnet had been an inspiration to her – she even served as the house's first creative director for a short time when it was resurrected in 2006, putting the technical craft back on the agenda.

The condensed idea
Technical marvel that fundamentally changed how clothing could be fitted

12 Polyester

Polyester is estimated to be one of the most widely used fibres in the world. It has also proved to be a polarizing invention for the fashion industry. On the one hand, it has brought benefits to consumers for its resilience, ease of care, ability to retain its shape, and its long-lasting nature – all pros for a fast-paced and rapid-moving modern world in which consumers are often time poor and cannot necessarily afford to keep buying. On the other hand, there are growing concerns about the negative effects of polyester on the environment and poor sustainability.

A synthetic fibre, polyester is generally made from acid and alcohols derived from petroleum, which is a fossil fuel. Petroleum is a non-renewable resource, which means it has a finite limit and poses difficulties when it comes to producing it and also disposing of it. Polyester does not biodegrade because it is a form of plastic and there are estimates that it takes many years (numbers vary from decades to centuries) for it to break down. And while it does so, it releases microplastics into the environment. All of these points have led the fashion industry to re-evaluate its relationship with what was once considered a miracle fabric.

Polyester is known for its durable, crease-resistant qualities, lightweight capabilities and an ability to dry quickly. It is also reasonably priced. It can typically be found in sportswear, performance clothes and summer dresses. It blends well with natural fabrics, such as cotton, which makes it a versatile material proposition.

> Polyester is the most popular material used in the fashion and textile industry. This reliance on virgin fossil-based materials is damaging to our environment, but there's no other fiber on the market today that could absorb this demand.
>
> textile exchange.org

History

There are various names and dates associated with the invention of polyester, which took place in the first half of the 20th century. In 1927, DuPont, the American multinational chemical company, coaxed

Dr Wallace Hume Carothers into leading its first decade of organic chemistry research. During April 1930, his team discovered neoprene synthetic rubber and synthesized the first polyester super polymer, which preceded nylon, also invented by Carothers in 1939. In 1941, J F Winfield and J T Dickson of the Calico Printers' Association, introduced a new fibre composition. By 1946, polyester fibres were used in the manufacture of home furnishings.

In fashion, it was used to make various kinds of items throughout the 1950s. Synthetics had become synonymous with affordable clothing and appealed to an emerging generation for whom a new era was defined by modernity and youth. Designers were keen to explore synthetics' aesthetics and properties, and manufacturers found them cost-effective alternatives to cotton and wool. Synthetics brought with them a sense of expendability for consumers who were keen to try out the latest fashions as they arrived.

Polyester can be a stretchy fabric. This is a benefit when it comes to sizing, but can also result in clothes clinging to the body more, which is sometimes less flattering. To the touch, it can be slightly coarse and scratchy. As a fabric, it tends to trap sweat, but can be washed easily, with little need for extra care.

Recycled polyester

In the last 20 years, the fashion industry has made concerted efforts to tackle the various environmental issues that come with producing – and over-producing – clothes. Among them has been a push to use

Nylon

Just like polyester, nylon was also developed by DuPont. It is a manufactured and man-made fibre that was introduced in the late 1930s. Its production is also reliant on fossil-fuel derived chemicals. Recycled nylon is also a possibility, using pre-consumer fabric waste or post-consumer material.

better and more environmentally considerate fibres and materials from the outset, and finding ways to reuse those already in circulation – especially those whose ecological footprint is not the most impressive.

Brands such as the outdoor clothing retailer Patagonia have been experimenting with recycling polyester (and claims that recycled polyester has been around since the 1990s). The retailer flags a statistic from the Textile Exchange: in 2022, the global production of polyester reached 63 million tonnes for the clothing industry alone. Using recycled polyester, it notes, reduces reliance on petroleum as a source of raw materials, utilizes waste and reduces greenhouse gas emissions from manufacturing. It also opens up new recycling streams for polyester clothing that is no longer wearable.

> Currently the industry is transitioning from virgin polyester to recycled polyester, in a bid to reduce its environmental impact and prevent waste.
>
> *Vogue* magazine

The industry is trying to transition from virgin polyester to recycled polyester. The aim is for brands to reduce their environmental impact and prevent waste. H&M, Adidas, and Zara's parent company Inditex are among those who set a target to ensure that 100 per cent of its polyester was recycled by 2025 and others are sure to follow. The move came as part of the Recycled Polyester Challenge from the Textile Exchange. The non-profit platform teamed up with the Fashion Industry Charter for Climate Action to launch it, as part of the United Nations Framework Convention on Climate Change.

Of course, polyester is not the only synthetic fabric. Nylon, also known for its long-lasting and durable qualities and with similar implications, is used widely in everything from underwear and stockings to tents.

New hope

In 2024, it was announced that a new polyester recycling plant had opened in the United Kingdom, at Kettering, Northamptonshire. It was a joint venture between the Salvation Army Trading Company Ltd (SATCoL) and Project Plan B. The plant recycles post-consumer garments, producing pellets from polyester waste. At the time of the news, in April, it was reported that the plant was on track

Not so chic

In 2018, an article in *The Guardian* newspaper – written as a documentary on Studio 54 was about to air – observed that polyester was a popular choice in the 1970s, but was banned at the famed nightclub during that time. Why? Because it was too deeply associated with the disco crowd and not the cool and chic clientele the nightclub owners wanted to attract. Polyester had a reputation for being poor quality and cheaply made; the environmental concerns surrounding it have only worsened its credentials.

to recycle 2,500 tonnes of unwanted polyester that year, with 5,000 tonnes the target for year two. The aim of the project is to save waste and return it to the supply chain – perhaps going some way in giving back polyester its miracle status after all…

The condensed idea
From miracle fabric to environmental hazard

13 Screen and digital print

Pop artists Andy Warhol and Roy Lichtenstein made screen printing famous in the art world, but it has had a significant role to play in the fashion world, too.

With a history that is thought to date back to the Song dynasty in China, 960–1279 CE, and further developed by other Eastern cultures, such as Japan, in subsequent centuries, screen printing is a process that involves a sort of stencilling technique for surface printing and it can be done by hand or by machine. Cloth is laid out on a printing table and the design applied through a screen made of silk or gauze that has been stretched over a frame. Print paste is poured onto the screen and spread out over the surface so that the colour is pushed through; the screen moves across the surface to ensure an even spread. Each colour is applied separately using different screens.

> The reason I'm painting this way is that I want to be a machine, and I feel that whatever I do and do machine-like is what I want to do.
>
> Andy Warhol

The invention of the screen-printing process provided the fashion industry with fabric in bulk, which was game-changing. Englishman Samuel Simon took out the first patent for a screen-printing process in 1907, and further patents followed. By the 1930s, screen-printing works were set up across Europe and the United States.

The process was relatively cheap and less labour-intensive as a method of printing cloth. But it accelerated production as it could respond quickly to changes in fashion trends. It also enabled designers to break free from the constraints of the expensive block-printing methods or engraved roller machines. As an innovation, it helped to democratize print design and transform fashion fabrics for the textile industry.

Renowned designers

Various contemporary designers have made a name for themselves through using screen printing. British designer Zandra Rhodes is particularly well known for her zigzag and butterfly prints, which often featured on kaftans and floating chiffon dresses. Having studied textile printing and lithography at Medway College of Art from 1959–61, she next went to the Royal College of Art, graduating in 1964. She is recognized as being a unique talent to emerge from the 1960s, owing to her distinct way of mixing texture and pattern, hand-screening many of her designs on chiffon and silk – something she still does today from her studio above Bermondsey's Fashion and Textile Museum, London. In 2019, the designer celebrated 50 years of design and has on and off shown her strikingly colourful creations at London Fashion Week.

In the mid-noughties, Scottish designer Jonathan Saunders put print and colour on fashion's agenda to renewed effect. Part of a new wave of exciting London fashion talent, the Central Saint Martins MA graduate quickly became known for his graphic and bright printed designs on slip dresses and A-line skirts, created using traditional screen-printing techniques. He made his debut at London Fashion Week for the autumn/winter 2003–4 season, winning a host of awards throughout his career. He would go on to become the creative director at Diane von Furstenberg – where screen-printing and strong, bold prints have always played a role – for a stint before closing down his label and moving into arts and interiors-based projects.

Printing methods

An effective way to decorate fabric using pigment and dyes, printing has its origins in antiquity. There is thought to be evidence of printing having occurred in India during the 4th century BCE with a printing block dated at around 300 CE. And pre-Columbian printed textiles have been found, it is reported, in Peru and Mexico. There are four main methods of textile printing: block, roller, screen and heat transfer. Textile printing has become a specialist skill and a sophisticated craft, used by designers in a multitude of ways. It is through printing that we have been able to bring patterns to clothes in a more timely fashion than embroidery, which is much more time-consuming.

Going digital

During this boom time in British fashion, something else was bubbling. In 2005, Bruno Basso and Christopher Brooke of the London-based fashion brand Basso & Brooke produced an entirely digitally printed collection. They had won the Fashion Fringe talent prize and thereafter showcased collections full of vivid and intense eye-dazzling patterns, inspired by travels and beyond. One of their pieces has made its way into the permanent collection at the Metropolitan Museum of Art, in New York. By 2010, they were no longer the only ones doing digital and it had become a popular pastime on the catwalk.

How does it work? Digital printing enables a designer to take an image directly from a camera or screen to the cloth, without involving the traditional silk-screening process, which, it is estimated, takes two to three months to complete. With digital printing, colours can be changed immediately, providing greater flexibility and the ability to trial countless variations before printing. It is a cost-effective method that can be easily printed onto luxury fabrics to create bespoke textiles. Prior to this, references to its use have been dated to the 1990s on synthetics.

Greek designer Mary Katrantzou, who graduated from Central Saint Martins in 2008, became known for her mesmerizing trompe l'oeil designs in the shape of perfume bottles and, later, riffing off interior design vistas, complete with lampshade peplums. She has worked with hyperrealistic prints and, as she has explained it, digital designs in a painterly sort of way, referring to her computer mouse as a paintbrush. Her collections are among those that stand out at this time for their use of digital printing, earning her the title 'queen of print' by the press.

> There was a big trend for bold digital prints at the time we launched our brand and we happened to be ready for it!
> Christopher de Vos and Peter Pilotto

Austrian-Italian Peter Pilotto and Belgian-Peruvian Christopher de Vos used digital prints when they launched their label in 2007. Having met while studying at the Royal Academy of Fine Arts in Antwerp, they did not set out to make prints their signature. However, they ended up using the technology to create vivid prints on sexy, draped and semi-futuristic dresses. It caught on, winning them critical acclaim.

More recently, the British fashion designer Richard Quinn, who launched his label in 2016, has promoted both printing techniques in his collections, which are known for their bold use of colour and pattern. He makes everything onsite from his studio in Peckham, London, with an Epson textile printer. The designer also offers both digital and screen-print services to fellow designers, from emerging to established.

The condensed idea
Handcraft versus technology

14 Sustainability

According to the Ellen MacArthur Foundation, each year millions of tonnes of clothes are produced, worn and thrown away. And, every second, the equivalent of a rubbish-truck-load of clothes is burned or buried in landfill.

In recent years, startling figures and statements such as these have become familiar to consumers. As ecological concerns about the planet have grown, so too have our concerns about the impact of fashion and what it does to the environment. Designers have started to take note and many build this into their business strategies, or use their brands as platforms to highlight environmental issues.

> I looked around me one day and realized that I knew nothing about where these clothes were made, and who made them. So, I started to educate myself and what I began to find was horrible.
>
> Arizona Muse, model

Meanwhile, consumers have started to rethink what and when they are buying for their wardrobes and from whom, considering elements such as the supply chain.

Sustainability in fashion is concerned with how it impacts the environment, including carbon footprints, water usage, chemicals, over-consumption and how the production of garments can cause as little harm to the environment as possible, as well as ethical issues surrounding the conditions of workers involved in the production line, their treatment and their pay. Sustainability can also take into consideration animal welfare and finding vegan alternatives.

Terminology

Terms frequently used in relation to sustainable fashion include 'upcycling', 'recycling', 'deadstock fabric', 'fair trade' and 'organic'.

Upcycling is when a discarded item of clothing is taken and transformed into something new, typically to elevate it in its current state. American designer Conner Ives makes dresses from T-shirts, for example. Recycling is when something is broken down and re-used to create something new. Various high-street brands now offer an option for you to take unwanted items in store. Deadstock fabric is leftover fabric, which is typically used for both upcycling and recycling purposes. Fair Trade relates to a trade agreement between companies in developed countries and producers in developing countries in which fair prices are paid to the producers. Organic generally refers to clothing made from natural fibres without the use of pesticides.

Changing trends

At the turn of the 21st century, talk of ethical and eco-friendly fashion was considered unfashionable and had associations with lesser-quality design. But this slowly started to change. Brands such as Edun, founded by U2 front man Bono and Ali Hewson, promoted the premise of trade for aid as a way to alleviate poverty through sustainable employment and growth. The handcrafted techniques focused on Africa and showed the best production from the continent. In 2009, the luxury group LVMH took a substantial share of the company. Though the whole operation ceased in 2018, the brand often showed during fashion week and conveyed how high fashion could engage with social and environmental causes.

Today most fashion brands are required to build a form of sustainability plan into their operations, be it their packaging, goals for the future to reduce waste, or an acknowledgement of some kind towards being responsible within the realms of selling product. This is largely down to consumers being better educated on the subject. During the 1990s, recycling became a societal sticking point in the United Kingdom, thanks to children's TV shows like *Blue Peter*.

Greenwashing

This term is used for when someone or something is making people believe it is doing more for the environment, or has more of an interest in it, than is actually the case. As the fashion industry gets to grips with the future of sustainability, various brands have been criticized as having greenwashed, or misled, consumers about their actions, or lack of them. There are various degrees of greenwashing, including the use of vague language.

Copenhagen Fashion Week

Sometimes described as the fifth fashion week, Copenhagen Fashion Week is defined by its focus on sustainability – its unique selling point. In 2020, it unveiled a three-year Sustainability Action Plan, outlining the requirements for brands to be a part of its schedule, and covering strategy as well as product. In order to qualify, at least 50 per cent of a designer's collection must be either certified, made of preferred materials or new generation sustainable materials, upcycled, recycled or made of deadstock. Collections are fur free, no single-use plastic can be used in packaging and the carbon footprint of the show must be offset. The plan is revised and released every three years.

Towards sustainable fashion

English designer Katharine Hamnett attended Central Saint Martins, graduating in 1970, and pushed for sustainability early on. She established her own brand in 1979 and became known for activist designs. In the early 1980s, she produced T-shirts printed with anti-war slogans and used her clothes to make the public aware of environmental as well as political issues. In 1989 she requested an audit into the environmental impact of her business and discovered how cotton production affects the environment and human lives. Devastated by the results, she decided it was time to change the way she worked and went on only to use organic and sustainable fabrics.

We need to stop making more stuff. Post Covid-19 we'll be facing a bigger environmental and inventory crisis than ever before; as people we overproduce, we over-consume and we waste too much.

Christopher Raeburn, designer

The late Vivienne Westwood started life as a punk pioneer, but soon channelled her efforts more into raising awareness for the environment and became an activist and campaigner, most notably through her Active Resistance to Propaganda (2007), a manifesto to save the planet for future generations and Climate Revolution (2012), an initiative to rally charities and NGOs together to engage political leaders.

Stella McCartney, a lifelong vegetarian, started her brand in 2001, having attended Central Saint Martins. The brand shows in Paris and is well known for its sophisticated tailoring and general feminine elegance. The brand does not use fur, feathers, leather or skins, none of which has hindered it from being successful.

Italian activist Livia Firth founded the Green Carpet Challenge in 2010. The idea was to pair glamour with ethics, putting sustainability on the red carpets of the world. Firth wore a series of sustainable gowns that awards season to promote environmental and social injustice, and invited high-profile actresses and designers to do the same. The Green Carpet Fashion Awards were launched subsequently, making sustainability more visible and glamorous than ever before.

The condensed idea
Sustainable fashion becomes a priority

15 3D Printing

n 2021, an updated article on the website refinery29.com asked, 'How far away are we from downloading our clothes?' It was pointing to one of the latest technological developments in the fashion industry: 3D printing.

For fashion, 3D printing is still a relatively new concept, despite having been clocked on catwalks back around 2010. It is also, for many, a game-changing concept that is capable of changing the way we both create and consume clothing.

3D-printing technology has been around since the 1980s, used often by engineers, architects and industrial designers to create prototypes. But what does it entail exactly? It is an additive form of manufacturing, which means an object can be created layer by layer, and involves heating plastic, or other materials such as metal and resin, to construct three-dimensional objects from digital models.

Origins

The XY plotter was the first idea for a 3D printer, patented by Hideo Kodama of the Nagoya Municipal Industrial Research Institute in 1981. Proposing the use of a photo-hardening thermoset polymer to create 3D models, it never got beyond being just an idea owing to funding constraints.

In 1984, French inventors Alain Le Méhauté, Olivier de Witte and Jean Claude André developed similar technology but a patent was abandoned. That same year, the first printing process debuted. It belonged to American Charles 'Chuck' Hull and his invention of a method in which a light source hardens polymer resin in thin layers to make 3D objects, coupled with his creation of the STL file type – the name given to a format that can describe the surface of an object via facets. When it was released in 1987, Hull's first printer, the SLA-1, was a landmark moment.

Understandably, as technology for 3D printing has evolved, it has become a fascinating tool for artists and designers to experiment with. London's Victoria and Albert Museum has various examples of its design works in its collections, from vases to furniture. Developments have led to 3D printing technology becoming more accessible and more affordable, with objects being built, or rather printed, quickly. The process also allows designers to produce one-off, custom pieces.

In fashion

As the noughties progressed, 3D printing started to garner serious interest as home printers debuted and the technology became more affordable. Fashion designers, including Alexander McQueen and Iris van Herpen, began to experiment with it. Shown in 2009, McQueen's spring/summer 2010 Plato's Atlantis collection was pertinent for two reasons. It was his last full collection (the designer died in 2010) and is thought to be one of his finest.

Referencing the sea-sunken island of Atlantis, described by Greek philosopher Plato, McQueen's collection featured exotic, vivid prints on shapes to match, as well as a distinctive 3D-printed Alien shoe. Otherworldly looking, the shoe was made from 3D-printed resin and featured a biomorphic snake design around the heel and a finger curling over the toes. Inspired by the artwork of H R Giger, a member of the special effects team for Ridley Scott's film *Alien*, in 1980, it looked both prehistoric and sci-fi futuristic, surely reinforced by its resin-printed structure. As a designer, McQueen is regarded as boundary pushing. He liked to shock and create drama through both his designs and collections, so it would make sense that he was among the early adopters of this new technology.

The well-known Dutch fashion designer Iris van Herpen is also a pioneer of 3D printing. During Paris Haute Couture week in 2011, she debuted a 3D-printed dress (an interesting if not provocative choice,

Download designs

In 2002, Nick Knight's SHOWstudio platform introduced a series called 'Design Download', in which it sought to democratize the fashion-making process. Designers, including John Galliano, Alexander McQueen and Yohji Yamamoto, offered their garment patterns for free so that viewers could download and interpret them, making for a different kind of early take on 3D printing.

given couture champions the touch of the hand). It was named among the year's best inventions by *Time* magazine. Van Herpen continues to use the method, which she first experimented with in 2009. She has noted that the first piece she printed took seven days to print, with each hour of every day being used.

The Guardian newspaper also wondered whether we were ready to print out our own 3D clothes back in 2015, and how wearable or comfortable such 3D fashion could be. In its article, it spot-lit the work of Israeli Danit Peleg, a fashion student who had made her graduate collection entirely through 3D printing. Rather than otherworldly, her aesthetic is fresh and sporty, and includes a red jacket, a crop top and skirt and a little mesh dress.

> **3D-printing has become a hot new tool in the fashion industry.**
> Liz Logan, *Smithsonian Magazine*

Further examples of 3D-printed fashion include New York-based Francis Bitonti, who printed a gown for Dita Von Teese in 2013 and, back on the couture catwalk, at Balenciaga for autumn/winter 2023. Georgian Demna Gvasalia debuted a Joan of Arc style ballgown constructed from 3D-printed resin and galvanized metal. It was a striking, if not haunting, design.

As part of his menswear offering for Louis Vuitton pre-fall 2024, Pharrell Williams sent a 3D-printed sneaker down the runway of his Hong Kong show, presented at the end of 2023. It was made using technology from a brand called Zellerfeld, which has also collaborated with the designer Heron Preston, the Danish label Rains and luxury fashion brand Moncler.

Pros and cons

As 3D printing moves manufacture from the hands of designers to those of consumers, concerns surrounding intellectual property have surfaced as the technology has evolved. There is also the consideration that it threatens artisanal handwork, a traditional and key element of the luxury sector, though specialist knowledge is typically required of 3D printing and there are still costs involved. Notably, the biggest issue is that 3D printing uses plastic, which is currently a difficult issue for fashion and sustainability. But, that said, others point out that being able to 3D print items as and when you need them would cut down on waste and that, as a process, it is actually very sustainable.

Speaking in refinery29.com's article, Muhammad Shahadat, from the Fashion Institute of Technology's digital centre in New York, thinks it could be a cure for fashion's over-consumption issue. It also has the potential, it has been suggested, to enable businesses to bypass large minimums required for factories, allowing them to produce in smaller numbers. For now, it certainly still grabs headlines.

The condensed idea
Fashion at your fingertips

16 Digital Fashion

Fashion is known for operating somewhat organically on a 20-year cycle. So, as the year 2020 approached, it is perhaps no wonder that there was once again interest in the potential of the online world. More than 20 years after the internet began dialling up, the fashion world was hit by a new phenomenon that had been brewing for some time: digital fashion.

Ever since video games existed, outfits for their characters existed, too. In some games, a player would have options to choose from (colours, maybe looks), others not. But as lockdowns persisted during to the Covid-19 pandemic, the idea of experimenting and getting dressed in a virtual world took off, especially since we could not enjoy the real one.

How it started

Digital fashion started to go mainstream with Nintendo's *Animal Crossing*, which debuted in 2001, but became popular owing to Instagram accounts such as Animal Crossing Fashion Archive and Nook Street Market. They made customized, or ode-to, designer outfits (also known as skins) available to players. Even the fashion designers Marc Jacobs and Valentino officially released looks for *Animal Crossing*'s New Horizons version.

In 2019, former *Harper's Bazaar* editor-in-chief Lucy Yeomans founded Drest, a metaverse-based styling community, in which players can attend events, shop a substantial selection of brands, and even dress supermodels. The idea had come to her in 2010, but she thought the fashion world was not quite ready for it. By 2020, things had changed.

> Fashion is about mixing and matching, customizing your garments and expressing your own unique identity.
>
> The Fabricant

Around this time, Louis Vuitton launched a League of Legends capsule collection in partnership with Riot Games, while Gucci was soon to debut a collaboration with The Sims. Burberry teamed up with Snapchat to create Animal Kingdom in which Snapcodes in store could transport shoppers to a Burberry world. Meanwhile,

NFTs

Non-fungible tokens (NFTs) were all anyone was writing about in the early 2020s. Fashion brands started to introduce them and the hype surrounding them was palpable. But what were they?

NFTs are digital tokens that exist on the blockchain (a type of ledger), and which cannot be replicated. They are the original item. Just like in couture, there is typically only one of anything. There can be replicas – or commercial ready-to-wear versions – but these are not the originals. An NFT certifies this authenticity and originality in the digital world, like a certificate of ownership. This started to appeal to fashion brands, certainly from a marketing point of view. In 2021, Dolce & Gabbana debuted five physical creations that also had virtual versions. Four other pieces were only digital. They sold for nearly $5.7 million. NFTs became the new collectibles, like futuristic antiques.

Balenciaga announced in 2020 that its autumn/winter 2021 collection would be presented by video game; *Afterworld: The Age of Tomorrow* imagined the world in 2031 and the Balenciaga clothes people would be wearing.

Social media was further escalating this fashion/digital-world crossover as more and more people were living their lives increasingly online, in part because of the pandemic and in part due to a general technological evolution. It made sense, then, to be able to express yourself stylistically as you would in real life. And the technology was emerging to back it up.

How it evolved

In 2019, the fashion house The Fabricant made headlines when it sold a digital dress – in other words, it was not physically real – for £7,500. Based in the Netherlands, The Fabricant is a digital fashion house formed in 2016–18 with the aim to create a decentralized fashion industry. Items come as NFTs, which can be traded with other players.

Around the same time as The Fabricant was Carlings, a Scandinavian fashion brand that catered to dressing your social media self. A collection called Neo-Ex debuted in 2018 and was fully digital and among the first of its kind. Experienced 3D designers adapted the pieces to consumers' photos of themselves so that you could be 'wearing' something that didn't physically exist. This brand new idea was not always understood. Indeed, NFTs caused similar problems. But the brand pointed out that tackling sustainability was key to their idea – digital fashion, they reasoned, cut down on shipping and overbuying. They had identified an emerging audience who bought skins for their virtual game characters and reasoned, with the rise of social media, that they may well want to do that for themselves too. Social media presented people with a new type of avatar. The Carlings collection sold out.

Meanwhile, DRESSX, founded in the United States by Daria Shapovalova and Natalia Modenova, offered a similar proposition, enabling users to buy and 'wear' digital garments from a selection of designers via a marketplace. Sustainability is also a key concern of the brand, which has collaborated with luxury fashion brands to digitize their garments.

The metaverse

A form of cyberspace, or virtual reality space, in which you can interact digitally via avatars or computer-generated environments with other users or players, the metaverse has been likened to a three-dimensional internet.

Think of it as being like the film Ready, Player One (2018). Certainly, the metaverse is the latest iteration of the internet, one that is no longer passive. For example, in 2020, 12 million players logged into a Travis Scott concert on the Epic Games video game Fortnite, while Lil Nas X's appearance on the gaming platform Roblox drew 33 million views. Neither of these were real-life events, but they confirmed the potential of the metaverse.

What are the benefits?

The rise of digital fashion has benefited emerging designers for whom the cost of creating collections has become more and more expensive – as has staging real-life fashion shows. Not only has it provided them with a means to show off their creativity, but it has encouraged them to be more creative. Colours, textures and fabric restrictions in the real world do not exist in the metaverse, which means a new generation of designers is able to imagine creations beyond the confines of those before them.

The movement has also come about in parallel to growing concerns about sustainability within the fashion industry and can be seen as a way to remedy it, encouraging people to buy less in real life. Of course, it works both ways and there are critics who feel digital fashion lacks the skills and craftsmanship of the hand, and that the energy required to create it still has an impact on the environment.

Personal style

Roblox, which debuted in 2004, is especially popular with Gen Z and Gen Alpha. The world-building game allows players to create environments and buy clothing for their characters from a marketplace – players can even upload their own designs. It means that anyone can now try their hand at being a fashion designer: the digital world of design has made fashion a more democratic place, full of a lot more ideas.

The condensed idea
Democratizing the industry by taking it somewhere new

17 Trends

I n the 2006 film, *The Devil Wears Prada*, based on the eponymous novel by Lauren Weisberger (2003), a poignant scene unfolds in the office of Miranda Priestly, played by Meryl Streep. Andrea Sachs, played by Anne Hathaway, snorts as the editor-in-chief of *Runway* magazine is picking out blue belts all of which, to Sachs, look the same.

Priestly is quick to give her a dressing down, pointing out that the 'lumpy' blue jumper she has on – in a shade of cerulean – is the result of a handful of designers who showed cerulean on the catwalk some seasons before. This, in turn, had been inspired by two particularly important uses of cerulean before them. The colour then got picked up by department stores, which then trickled down to Sachs' wardrobe. Priestly expressly says that it is because of the people in the room in which she is standing that Sachs is wearing that blue sweater.

> Florals? For spring?
> Groundbreaking.
> Miranda Priestly

This is one way that trends work. The trickle-down effect, from top to bottom, or the upper classes to the lower classes, and, in this instance, from high fashion to high-street fashion. This phenomenon has occurred throughout history.

The 20-year cycle

It is widely accepted that there is a 20-year rule in fashion trends. It takes 20 years for something to come back into fashion. The 1990s, for example, riffed off the 1970s. Now, in the 2020s, the 2000s are seeing a revival, with more hallmarks of the low-rise-jean era being reintroduced all the time, among them patchwork, diamante, asymmetric tops and handkerchief hems. What's next? Perhaps take a look back at what happened in the latter half of the 2000s – maybe Balmain's broad shoulders (2007) and Yves Saint Laurent's Tribute platform (2009), or London's New Rave scene (circa 2005 onwards).

The 15th-century Duke of Burgundy, Philip the Good, is said to have set the trend for wearing black on the death of his father, John the Fearless, in 1419. The Belle Epoque era towards the end of the 19th century was a time of expansion and was fairly peaceful. The upper classes indulged in leisure pursuits that those lower down the social hierarchy would aspire to. And when Alexandra of Denmark, the wife of King Edward VII, wore a choker and high neckline, the look became widely copied. Bringing glamour to the royal family, she became a focus of high society.

Trends govern what we do, what we like and what we wear (a boom in loungewear during the pandemic, for example. . .). They also make us push against them (. . .that we never wanted to touch again once the pandemic was over). The word 'trend' describes a change or development that leads something to become popular, fashionable and copied by many. Why is it that one colour is suddenly everywhere? That wide-leg trousers are in every shop? That everyone is wearing a certain sort of sandal? Where do these ideas come from?

How do trends get decided?

The answer to this question is constantly changing, especially since the advent of social media. There was a time when trends were born every six months with little intervention between. They were dictated by designers and industry insiders: catwalk shows took place behind closed doors; magazines would decide what to write about; a trend would be declared for short hemlines. Today, trends are born overnight. They go 'viral' and do not even need the catwalk to launch or promote them. TikTok and Instagram now have the power to unleash a forgotten fashion item back into life or stir up a sudden left-field craze, as was seen with the 'mob wife' chic of 2024.

Fashion academic Elizabeth Wilson points out that after the Industrial Revolution, life was no longer organized around the agricultural calendar. The same can be said of the digital or social revolution of the internet. It has destabilized the fashion cycle – it has also democratized it – and we no longer live to six-month fashion seasons. The internet also serves an archive of readily accessible imagery and design that gives consumers the ability to pick and choose what they want. The rise of second-hand clothes and vintage means they do not even have to shop in the same decade anymore.

Street style

Street style has become a new resource for trend hunting, uncovering personal and individualistic takes on fashion. While on the catwalk red might be popular, the streets of London may point to something else – as, equally, might the streets of a fashion week outside of the big four. Fashion publications will now often produce a round-up of street-style trends just as much as they do the catwalk collections.

Furthermore, a growing emphasis on sustainability has created an anti-trend movement, in a similar way to grunge and subcultures' rejection of the mainstream. In the case of streetwear, it ended up inspiring designers at the top, reversing the trickle-down theory.

Elsewhere, the emergence of fast fashion has meant that it is quick, cheap and easy to copy the look of a favourite celebrity on a whim. Celebrities, be they aristocrats from the grand courts of times past or influencers of today, have always played a role in disseminating trends. In the modern, socially connected world, fans have more access to their role models than ever before. When Taylor Swift was spotted wearing a £58 green velvet dress by the Scottish brand Little Lies, it promptly sold out.

Trend forecasters

Trends can work on both a micro and a macro scale. Micro refers to smaller niche shifts in patterns, while macro considers the broader landscape. Trend forecasters will work to predict the latter.

Corporate businesses often enlist the services of trend forecasters to future-proof themselves. WGSN, The Future Laboratory and Edelkoort are among the best-known trend-forecasting agencies.

WGSN (Worth Global Style Network) was founded in 1998 and is based in 38 cities across six continents. Using data analytics and global expert insights, it works in the lifestyle and fashion sectors to predict consumer behaviour and trends. The Future Laboratory started in 2000 with a team of two and a handful of clients, but has now advised more than 1,000 businesses in 50 countries. It helps clients to understand emerging consumer needs and how to position their brands. Dutch trend forecaster Lidewij Edelkoort has been predicting trends since the 1980s and is one of the world's

When Lidewij Edelkoort started her career as a trend forecaster 45 years ago, people thought her job was 'witchcraft', she says.
The Guardian

most famous forecasters. She founded her company in Paris in 1991, operating as a think-tank, or research institute. In 1998 she created *Bloom* magazine, the first magazine of its kind to examine trends in horticulture in relation to fashion, interior design, architecture and more.

The condensed idea
Trends come and go. . .and come back again

18 Fashion Schools

Yves Saint Laurent famously apprenticed with Christian Dior in 1955, going on to become his assistant in 1957. Alexander McQueen's CV includes stints as an apprentice for Savile Row tailors Anderson & Sheppard and Gieves & Hawkes. Meanwhile, some of fashion's biggest names can be found among the alumni of the London College of Fashion, Central Saint Martins and Royal College of Art, or Parsons and the Fashion Institute of Technology (FIT), both in New York, or Antwerp's Royal Academy of Fine Arts, among others.

It is through teaching, be it in the classroom or in the atelier, that the knowledge of creating fashion and its accompanying skill set are handed down. And it is because of the names that pass through the doors that aspiring young designers find themselves dreaming of attending the very same institutions. Often, fashion designers guest-lecture at universities to share their knowledge of the industry. Others, following a successful career in the industry, return to education to teach new generations of students. There are various ways to enter the fashion industry to become a designer, maker or craftsperson (as well as, increasingly, a fashion journalist or buyer).

> I've always believed that you have to have the skills before you destroy the skills.
>
> Louise Wilson

Apprenticeships

The concept of the apprenticeship as a way in which to enter working life has existed since medieval times in Europe. Historical texts are reported to show that craftspeople who focused on specific trades were members of guilds as early as 1156 in the United Kingdom. Out of these guilds came trade associations called livery companies, which emerged at various times. They include the Worshipful Company of Goldsmiths, the Worshipful Company of Dyers and the Worshipful Company of Cordwainers, among others. They were founded to regulate the trade of their specialism and supported apprenticeships, just as they continue to do today. During the 19th and 20th centuries, women would often apprentice for jobs in millinery and dressmaking, while men would be taught manual trades.

Apprenticeships are a traditional and established route into working in the garment industry, usually with a structured training plan. Work experience often takes place for shorter stints of time and is more common in the fashion industry as opposed to Savile Row. It enables a student to develop skills, both practical and social, to put on their CV in order to seek an entry-level employment position.

The best-known of apprenticeships in the UK fashion world are those on Savile Row, London's hub of menswear tailoring. Besides McQueen – another well-known designer to have gone through an apprenticeship here is Stella McCartney.

In the classroom

The teaching of fashion as a subject in schools, colleges and universities is something that has only really taken hold over the past 100–150 years internationally. Fashion historian Christopher Breward has noted that fashion design was recognized as a subject worthy of serious study relatively late on, but that there were tailoring academies in the 1870s and local-authority-funded trade schools opened at the turn of the century. Private needlecraft and drawing schools existed around the same time.

During the 20th century, there came the founding and recognition of the now legendary fashion schools and pioneering teachers. During the 1960s, it was under Janey Ironside at London's Royal College of Art that key designers of the 1960s, such as Ossie Clark and Sally Tuffin of Foale and Tuffin, were schooled. Mary Quant, meanwhile, had gone to Goldsmiths and graduated a decade earlier.

The famous schools

Central Saint Martins (CSM) started out as two colleges founded in the 19th century: St Martin's School of Art and the Central School of Art and Crafts, which became the Central School for Art and Design in 1966. They both shared the same ethos, which is little changed

Louise Wilson

Both terrifying and talented, Louise Wilson was the hugely respected head of the Central Saint Martins MA fashion course. Holding the position for 22 years, she mentored many of the world's leading names in fashion, including Phoebe Philo, Christopher Kane, John Galliano, Alexander McQueen, Jonathan Saunders, Simone Rocha and Roksanda Ilincic. It was Wilson who managed to get the end-of-year student show onto the official schedule of London Fashion Week, making it one of the most hotly anticipated shows of the year, its audience full of talent spotters ready to find fashion's next new star. They frequently did.

Wilson, who died at the age of 52 in May 2014, was known for her sharp eye and sharper tongue. She had a passion for fashion education and cared for her students who, for the most part, feared her for all the right reasons. She pushed them to come up with the best and most exciting ideas, putting London fashion on the map. Many have said since her passing that she was the most influential figure in their life. In honour of her legacy, the Louise Wilson MA fashion fund was set up, an initiative enabling students to study on the course regardless of their background.

today, believing in the importance of learning through making and taking a radical approach to art and design. In 1989, the two colleges merged to form Central Saint Martins, which is part of the University of the Arts, London (UAL), alongside the London College of Fashion, which was founded in 1906.

The Royal College of Art (RCA) was originally the Government School of Design in 1837, but was granted a royal charter and university status in 1967. Besides fashion designers such as Zandra Rhodes and Ossie Clark, it produced the artists Barbara Hepworth, Henry Moore, Peter Blake and David Hockney. During the 1990s, it produced the fashion designers Philip Treacy, Julien Macdonald, Christopher Bailey, Alice Temperley and Andrew Fionda.

Among the most highly regarded fashion schools in Europe is The Royal Academy of Fine Arts in Antwerp, founded in 1663, which gave the fashion world Glenn Martens of Y/Project and Diesel, Demna Gvasalia of Vetements (from 2014–19) and Balenciaga, and the 80s fashion collective, the Antwerp Six.

In New York, Parsons School of Design and the Fashion Institute of Technology (FIT), opening in 1896 and 1944 respectively, have given us: (Parsons) Anna Sui, Marc Jacobs, Donna Karan, Tracy Reese and (FIT) Michael Kors, Calvin Klein, Norma Kamali, Bibhu Mohapatra, Luke Meier (of Jil Sander), Daniel Roseberry and Ralph Rucci.

The condensed idea
Skills and knowledge passed down

19 The Department Store

Selfridges, Harrods, Le Bon Marché, Galeries Lafayette, Macy's, Saks Fifth Avenue. . .With their beauty halls and food halls, book departments and Christmas departments, womenswear, menswear and childrenswear-dedicated floors, technology spaces and pop-up corners, and seasonal window displays – not to mention, for some, fine jewellery offerings, repair services, restaurants and cafes – department stores are often a sight for the senses: one-stop shops and places of entertainment and fantasy.

Department stores are churches of consumerism for worshippers of merchandise, enabling them to see a host of ideas and items under one roof without having to step outside into the elements. A relatively modern phenomenon, most have roots in the 19th century, though there is evidence to suggest their existence, and their influence, dates back to the late 18th century. Typically, they began life as large haberdasher's that started to expand their businesses by consolidating various goods that previously would have been sold in separate stores, and introducing services. But it was during a boom across Britain, Europe and the United States in the 19th century that saw them change the course of shopping.

Englishman Emerson Muschamp Bainbridge is namechecked early on as opening a store in Newcastle Upon Tyne in 1838. Sometimes referred to as the earliest department store, by 1849, it is said to have had 23 departments. Before that, in 1796, Harding, Howell & Co at

---

Show and sell

The fashion historian Christopher Breward has pointed out that publicity and presentation are an important currency upon which the fashion retail industry has relied since the emergence of the late-modern clothing industry in the 19th century. He also states that the shop is the last stage in a garment's production/promotion lifespan.

89 Pall Mall was divided into four departments that offered furs and fans, haberdashery, jewellery, clocks and millinery.

Le Bon Marché, which lays claim to being the first department store to open in Paris, came along in 1852; La Samaritaine, also in Paris, was founded in 1870, Galeries Lafayette in 1912; in London, Harrods was established in 1849 (having started out as grocer in 1834), Whiteleys from 1863, and arguably the most famous of them all, Selfridges in 1909. Other names to note are Harvey Nichols, Liberty, Marks & Spencer, John Lewis, Bergdorf Goodman, Bloomingdale's, Nordstrom and Printemps.

> There wasn't much not to like. The place was a marvel. There were six acres of floor space with no internal doors.
>
> Lindy Woodhead, *Shopping, Seduction & Mr Selfridge*

Over the years, the department store has played an important role in the promotion of fashion. It has also helped to democratize it. The New York department store Bloomingdale's, for example, was one of the first to organize fashion departments that enabled designers to show their clothes in a boutique-style environment. Today, it is the department store that houses luxury brands that perhaps do not have stores locally, bringing both new and established names to customers.

And, with all its multi-facets and different reasons to shop, the department store can also be seen as more hospitable perhaps than a dedicated store, and less intimidating. This was certainly the case during the 19th century for women.

Women

As women were granted greater social reforms, shopping became a leisure activity in which they could partake. Major cities were becoming home to department stores, which offered a safe space for women to browse and to meet friends, unchaperoned by a man – at a time they typically needed to be accompanied by one. The woman was no longer bound by her home. This was a significant development. Beyond being a place to shop, the department store was therefore a place of freedom. Cloakrooms, tearooms and lavatories were added towards the end of the 19th century. Customers were not obligated to buy as they perused inside these lavish premises; everything was there for them to enjoy.

The concept store

A modern and more curated interpretation of the department store is the concept store, which has taken its kudos and luxury products and made them even more exclusive. Interior design might be borderline inhospitable, intimidating and progressive, or kooky and fun, featuring artworks and installations that connect the product to a world beyond that of fashion – which is mostly the point.

Dover Street Market, London, the brainchild of Rei Kawakubo of Comme des Garçons, opened on the eponymous street in 2004. Its industrial interior design with concrete floors and narrow staircases, was home to new and exciting names. It felt like an exclusive fashion world with a mix of streetwear and high fashion. It has since expanded and moved to new premises in London, and has stores across the world.

Spectacles

So lavish were the interiors during the early iterations that department stores gained a reputation as tourist attractions for people to visit. This is still true today, as a day out in London, Paris and New York is hardly complete without a visit to its landmark stores.

A great deal of design and effort goes into creating an enjoyable shopping experience. Attention is given to changing rooms, to walkways, to finishes and hangers, rails and payment points; how it feels to walk from one section to another; the overall experience as well as the product on offer. How do you feel when you enter? How do you feel when you leave? All of these things help decide where a department store sits in the retail hierarchy and it is a very competitive retail world.

In London, Harrods has made headlines for collaborations with brands such as Dior to create gingerbread vistas, displayed like museum exhibits. Harvey Nichols and Selfridges are well known for their window displays and pop-up initiatives, such as a nostalgic joke shop at the latter in recent years, which is also well known for its founder, the American Harry Gordon Selfridge.

Selfridges

The most famous of names when it comes to department stores is Selfridges and that of Harry Gordon Selfridge. He was the son of a small shopkeeper in Wisconsin and, aged 21, joined the wholesale-retail company Field, Leiter & Company, in Chicago. He worked there for 25 years, before becoming a junior partner and, in 1906, left for England to build a large department store on Oxford Street. The store opened in 1909 with a floor space of 42,000 square feet. Selfridge was particularly good at advertising, publicity and creating captivating interiors, all of which helped to make the department store a household name. And today it is recognized globally.

An American who had ventured into department stores before this was John Wanamaker, who took the idea to the United States in 1875–76 and bought a rail-freight depot in Philadelphia, filling it with speciality retailers. He is said to have innovated price tags and was known for his aggressive advertising.

The condensed idea
A place for women, a place for ideas

20 The Fashion Show

During the autumn/winter 2024 season, the fashion show everyone was talking about was Louis Vuitton – it was Nicolas Ghesquière's 10th anniversary as creative director at the famed Parisian house. And it was a triumph. Not only because the collection once again tapped so successfully into his greatest hits at the house, and his affinity for sci-fi, but because it put on a real show – for 4,000 or so guests. The press hailed it as the return of the megawatt show.

Megawatt shows have become the currency of fashion brands. The late Karl Lagerfeld, while at the helm of Chanel, routinely put on fashion shows that rivalled film sets. There was a beach, there was a spaceship, there was a supermarket. And resort/cruise and pre-collections (those shown between the two main seasons, catering for holidays and winter wardrobe gaps) have become big business in recent years, taking place in beautiful, far-flung and Instagrammable destinations such as Seoul, Shanghai, Los Angeles and Rio de Janeiro.

The fashion show functions as a press-facing vehicle for selling clothes, providing the designer with a means for showcasing a creative and compelling vision for their fashion house. Lately, the aim has also been to 'go viral'. The fashion show is therefore also about promotion. At couture shows, the intention is to sell the clothes directly to

Teamwork

A complex event, a fashion show can cost hundreds of thousands, even millions, of pounds to produce. Aside from the clothes, it requires a venue, models, a production team, make-up artists and hair stylists, lighting and sound engineers, music, dressers, security and a PR team. It also requires guests – the fashion press, buyers for stores, celebrities who sit in the front row, friends and family, and now, of course, influencers. Months of hard work go into a show that will typically last only 10 to 20 minutes. While the show itself might be relatively short, however, its impact will be lasting.

Supermodels

The 1990s is regarded as the era of the 'supermodel', one claiming they would not wake up or get out of bed for less than $10,000 a day. The 'supers' included Naomi Campbell, Christy Turlington, Cindy Crawford, Linda Evangelista and Tatjana Patitz, as well as Kate Moss, whose waif-like figure came in contrast to the strong, svelte and athletic bodies of the more typical supers. Other names included Stephanie Seymour, Helena Christensen, Eva Herzigova, Claudia Schiffer and Tyra Banks. They walked the big shows in an era of big brands and they made big money.

customers, the privileged few who sit in the front row and make orders each season. But it is through the magic of couture that the myth and allure of the brand excels. Promotion, once again.

Origins

The earliest fashion shows used to be intimate and closed-off events, intended only for the few, such as press, buyers, celebrities and private clients, not the masses. This has always been part of their appeal (although, in 1984, Thierry Mugler allowed people to buy tickets to his show).

Charles Frederick Worth, noted as the father of couture, played a key role in the development of the fashion show. He is credited as being the first designer to use live models – the female shop assistants – instead of mannequins to show his clothing in the mid-1800s (though real models were often referred to as mannequins). Among them was his wife, Marie Vernet.

Paul Poiret, noted as one of the designers who helped to free women from the constraints of the corset, is also known for his promotion tactics. He would devise spectacular parties or events as a backdrop to the showing of his seasonal collections. And around 1912, he organized a series of touring fashion shows across Europe and then the United States.

The fashion designer Lady Duff-Gordon, of Lucile, was known to show collections regularly at her Hanover Street salon (some say she

One legendary fashion show was held in 1973, when five French and five American designers pitted their talents against one another (apparently, *WWD*'s editor John B Fairchild called it the Battle of Versailles). Held at the Théâtre Gabriel, the event was organized to raise money for Versailles palace, which required restoration. The French couturiers were Marc Bohan for Christian Dior, Pierre Cardin, Hubert de Givenchy, Yves Saint Laurent and Emanuel Ungaro. The American guests were Bill Blass, Stephen Burrows, Oscar de la Renta, Halston, and Anne Klein. A fashion-show-meets-cabaret extravaganza, it put American sportswear up against French couture. It also championed diversity: of the 36 American models, 10 were African American, as was one of the designers. Though there seems to have been no real 'winner' of the event, it is widely thought that the Americans stole the show – which at the time seemed quite the surprise.

was the first), while department stores would also start to host in-store shows from around the 1910s and 1920s. The fashion parade started to become a thing in the early 20th century.

Fashion week

The PR whizz attributed as being the first-ever fashion publicist, Eleanor Lambert instigated New York Fashion Week. At a time when American fashion designers were largely overlooked for their European counterparts, Lambert worked to put them on the map. In 1943, what would become the first New York Fashion Week was held under the umbrella of Press Week. Lambert set up shows at the Pierre Hotel and the Plaza. The events of World War II prevented the American press from travelling to Europe to see designers, so this became an opportunity to promote home-grown talent. Today, a mix of established and emerging names show at New York Fashion Week, which is known to be the most commercial of the four. London is known for a distinct blend of creativity; Milan for tradition; and Paris for setting the trends.

After the war ended, the French fashion industry needed help. It was the son of couturier Nina Ricci, Robert, who had an idea to invite fashion houses to create mini versions of their designs for Le Petite Théâtre de la Mode, which went on show at the Louvre before touring around Europe in a special and very petite sort of fashion show.

In 1958, in an attempt to compete with the shows of Paris, Italy set up its Camera Nazionale della Moda Italiana, making Milan the centre of the fashion show. And, in 1960, a group of designers including Carven and Nina Ricci began to show their ready-to-wear collections two weeks before the couture collections. Showing ready-to-wear on a catwalk became the new way to do things. The birth of Paris Fashion Week came in 1973.

The magic of a show

The location of a fashion show says much about the designer and the brand. Cool and edgy designers have the ability to show in equally cool and edgy venues – Alexander McQueen was known for luring the fashion press to the depths of London's East End at a time when it had not yet been made over by artisanal coffee shops and organic wine stores. Meanwhile, Vetements has often made an audience go to the outskirts of Paris, or sex clubs, to see the fruits of its latest collections. Also important is who walks in the show – specifically which model opens and closes it. These are usually the most exciting names in fashion, whether new, established or legendary.

Anyone who has been to a fashion show will tell you there is nothing quite like it. The sense of anticipation, the red rope being lifted for you to enter, taking your seat surrounded by chatter until, suddenly, the lights go down low, the music blares and the first look exits. Photographers at the pit at the end of the catwalk click away as the models walk into a sea of flashes and the moment is captured. It has only been since the dawn of social media that the fashion show has been opened up to the world, with collections transmitted in seconds online so that even if you are not there you can be, of sorts.

The condensed idea
Fashion promotion

21 Fashion Magazines

Fashion magazines, today glossy to the touch (and thus referred to as 'glossies'), aspirational and impactful in their cover star choices, and inviting in their assertive and confident coverlines, have experienced a difficult time as the 21st century has been growing accustomed to developments in technology.

Nevertheless, magazines have long played – and continue to do so – a pivotal role in documenting trends and fashions of the time, introducing designers of note and creating photographic shoots that transport readers into different worlds. There is also a lot of money to be made from advertising in fashion magazines, which is largely how they are funded, as opposed to the sales of their issues, circulation of which has dwindled in recent times. Yet, to utter the word *Vogue* still carries much clout and authority.

The role of the fashion magazine has been to bring together the words of fashion writers and features editors and images – often a collaboration between photographers and stylists/fashion editors – to inform the reader about what is in fashion and what is not, what to wear and how to wear it. Readers discover new trends (originally dictated by fashion magazines) and learn what they should buy and when. Fashion magazines instil a sense of desire in the reader and bring fashion to popular consciousness.

Dedicated fashion magazines date back to the late 18th century in England and France and became especially popular in the 19th century. Hand in hand with industrial developments of the time, such as the sewing machine, they contributed to the democratization of fashion for which there was becoming an increased appetite.

Vogue

Of all the fashion magazines, *Vogue* is probably the most widely known. It started in the United States, in 1892, as a weekly fashion magazine aimed at society women. Purchased in 1909 by Conde Nast, it then became twice monthly. In 1914, Edna Woolman Chase was appointed editor of American *Vogue*. A British edition launched in 1916 with the British-born William Wood as proprietor, manager and managing editor. By 1920, the first issue of French *Vogue*

Fashion illustration

Though rarified in its use now, fashion illustration pre-dates photography as the mode to show the latest fashions in journals and magazines. In 1908, Paul Iribe was commissioned to illustrate the fashion designs of Paul Poiret for a small promotional publication called *Les Robes de Paul Poiret*, which marked a move away from the stilted poses presented in drawings prior to this. The images were bold and stylized with an orientalist feel and set a new trend for fashion illustration. They were especially popular during the 1930s, known as fashion plates, but as fashion photography started to creep in, as a medium fashion illustration was pushed out. Today, it is a specialist form that appears more often in exhibitions than it does in magazines.

appeared. Subsequent editions of the magazine launched in Spain, Germany and Australia.

Over the years *Vogue* magazine has been celebrated for its fantastical shoots by famous photographers such as Cecil Beaton and Lord Snowdon, and its fierce editors, from Diana Vreeland to Anna Wintour, upon whom the novel *The Devil Wears Prada*, published in 2003, is supposed to be based. In 2017, Ghanaian-born British Edward Enninful became the first Black man to edit the publication, exiting in 2024 after six years. He is credited with diversifying the magazine, which had typically been thought of as being for upper-middle class women until his tenure.

Harper's Bazaar

Launched by Fletcher Harper, of the US publisher Harper & Brothers, in 1867, *Harper's Bazar* (originally with one 'a') started life as a women's magazine that covered the home as well as fashion. Until 1901 it was published weekly, then went monthly. It was bought by the Hearst publishing empire in 1913 and, in 1929, the second 'a' was added to the title making it 'Bazaar'. The magazine has always been seen as a rival to *Vogue*, with many a fashion editor and photographer poached and swapped between the two over the years. Carmel Snow,

Fashion photography

The origins of fashion photography can be traced back to Victorian-era portraiture, when debutantes and performers posed for photographers in the same way that people posed for portrait artists previously. The early 20th century saw a rise in fashion photography in magazines, owing to advances in the development of effective ways to reproduce the images. It also helped that fashion magazines themselves were becoming more widely available at this time.

Fashion photography has been seen as a way to sell dreams, not just clothes. Where illustration may have documented details, photography created mood, desire and aspiration. Styles of fashion photography were also reflective of the times – surrealism took off in the 1920s and 1930s, for example, and is captured in the innovative and challenging fashion photography of the era.

a keen promoter of fashion design, photography and illustration, is among its revered editors. Diana Vreeland, who would also work for *Vogue*, worked at *Harper's Bazaar* and is best known for her outspoken fashion mantras.

WWD

Originally a trade journal, meaning it was targeting the clothing industry as opposed to a consumer audience, *Women's Wear Daily*, commonly abbreviated to *WWD*, was converted into a magazine (and today, is also a website) that appealed to both by a man named John Fairchild, who became its publisher in 1960. Fairchild worked for Fairchild Publications, which was founded by his grandfather Edmund Fairchild. In 1954, John spent time in Paris as a reporter, where he put his own stamp on the genre of fashion journalism.

He filed gossipy stories and broke embargoes (which stipulate an approved date on which a story can run) in a move that brought a new lively format to the publication. He took over as publisher of *Women's Wear Daily* in 1960 and became chief executive of Fairchild Publications. He also launched the titles *W* and *M* for those he had dubbed 'the beautiful people' – one among many of the memorable phrases that are credited to him when talking about the people in fashion, and the world of fashion in general.

Style titles

The antithesis of the glossy fashion magazine is the subcultural style magazine: edgy, alternative, underground, authentic and typically independent. Titles such as *i-D*, *The Face*, *Sleazenation* and, for a time, *Vice* grew up in the 1980s and 1990s as a counter to the culture of the more conservative glossy magazines. They often started out as zines or music listings and have become significant in their grass-roots approach to documenting culture and promoting originality. Walk into a newsagent today, and you will be greeted by an abundance of fashion publications, something for everyone.

The condensed idea
Selling dreams
as well as clothes

22 Fashion and the Screen

The Golden Age of Hollywood is attributed to the 1930s, when leading ladies of the screen also became leading ladies of fashion. Fashion historian Elizabeth Wilson compares it to being like the spectacle of the royal courts. Their influence was great, and their glamour even greater. Indeed, going to the cinema was big business and reached mass audiences, which in turn meant that Hollywood style spread far and wide too – in mass-produced fashions for the woman on the street. Everyday women wanted to look like their heroines, whose style had been carefully cultivated by the movie studios.

Hollywood

Blonde bombshells of the Golden Age of Hollywood included Mae West, Carole Lombard and, later, Marilyn Monroe. During the 1930s, the black-and-white nature of the screen made the imagery it showed all the more alluring and seductive, and the fashions, therefore, all the more powerful. As a result, it has been suggested that Hollywood contributed to an overarching trend of consumerism in America.

In those days, it was the stars who set the trends, whereas it has been argued that the stars of today follow existing trends – you are more likely to see a dress on the runway and then a celebrity wearing it rather than the other way round, for example. And it was through the stars that women learned about fashion – oftentimes more so than

The red carpet

Not only do films and their characters provide much in the way of fashion inspiration, the medium provides another catwalk opportunity: the red carpet, which quickly translates into 'Get the look' shopping pages in magazines and Instagram posts. Award-show outfits and trends are dissected by both the public and fashion pundits, often with versions quickly offered up by the high street. Red has been a big hit of late, as has the 'naked' dress or wearing knickers visibly.

through the pages of magazines like *Harper's Bazaar* and *Vogue*, particularly before they were widely circulated.

It has been reported that, in 1932, the New York department store Macy's sold 500,000 copies of a white dress that boasted huge flounced sleeves and that had been worn by a then 26-year-old Joan Crawford in the film *Letty Lynton* of the same year. The original dress had been designed by the costume designer Adrian, whose name is now synonymous with Hollywood costume, a legend in the field who was pivotal in joining the dots between the worlds of film and fashion. Previously, Paris had dictated the high-fashion trends of the time but now Hollywood had a role in influencing the masses.

Adrian

No other name in the history of costume design is as well known as Adrian, whose rule during the Golden Age of Hollywood is the stuff of fashion dreams. Born in 1903, in Naugatuck, Connecticut, he studied at the School of Fine and Applied Arts, New York (now The New School, Parsons), and in Paris. He designed costumes for Broadway shows until 1925, when he headed to Hollywood to make clothes for Rudolph Valentino.

He worked for DeMille Studios from around 1926–28, and soon after became chief costume designer at Metro-Goldwyn-Mayer. It was while here that he designed for Greta Garbo – an icon for many women – for many years. The 'slouch' hat he made for Garbo's character in the film *A Woman of Affairs* (1928) is said to have influenced fashion for at least a decade. Another highly copied style was an ostrich-feather-trimmed hat, featured in the film *Romance* (1930), that partially obscured the eye. His pillbox hat for Garbo's character in *As You Desire Me* (1932) also set trends. It is Adrian who is credited with giving Joan Crawford her signature look – with wide, padded shoulders that worked to make the hips look smaller – and Jean Harlow's look, where slinky dresses that hugged the figure were cut on the bias.

Adrian semi-retired from cinema in 1942 and opened a shop in Beverly Hills, where he continued to make garments for films and to sell his own fashions, until his death in 1959. Particular signatures of his work include bias-cut evening gowns and bold silhouettes. Remarkably, he never won an Oscar – but that was because he retired before the awards were ever given out.

As Seen On Screen

In 2000, British businessman Nick Robertson founded As Seen On Screen, better known by its acronym, ASOS. Launched at a time when reality TV was starting to emerge and celebrity interest was high, the company sold replica goods and fashion that had been seen on celebrities in film and on TV. Its focus purely on fashion came a little later, leading it to become a global powerhouse, with reportedly more than 18 million customers in 238 countries, selling copycat looks of red carpet and onscreen looks. Though it would go on to add its offering with a market-place and carry other brands.

This was not a new concept, however. Back in the 1930s, the US ready-to-wear industry, which became a hub of mass manufacture, was producing copies of the pieces that featured in films. Star-endorsed styles were sold through the advertising agent Bernard Waldman's Modern Merchandising Bureau and chain of Cinema Fashion Shops, of which there were 400 by 1937.

Ahead of a given film release, sketches or photographs of the looks the actresses were going to wear in the movie would be sent to the bureau and the clothes reproduced. Typically, they would be less extreme than the original versions, which were often exaggerated for the screen. Fabrications were not of the same high quality either; rayon was a useful replacement for silk, for example.

Sex and The City

When the HBO TV series *Sex and The City* debuted in 1998, no one could have foreseen how much of an impact it would have on our own wardrobes. Until this point, no TV show had dictated trends or been the inspiration for shopping pages in magazines. Now, everyone wanted Carrie Bradshaw's wardrobe – the clothes in it and the walk-in setup itself – which had been curated by the costume designer Patricia Field, whose power lay in her ability to delve into past eras and source vintage finds that weren't on sale on the high street – not yet, anyway.

Field curated a sense of style that had not been seen before and brought to life the eclectic and complicated world of four singletons living in Manhattan in the late 1990s and early 2000s. Manolo Blahnik, the luxury footwear label, would be the most referred to fashion brand in the show, prompting a rush to own a pair of the designer's shoes. There have been other impactful series, such as *Emily in Paris* (also

Notable names associated with costume for film are Travis Banton, Howard Greer, Orry-Kelly and Edith Head. These people were not deemed couturiers in the traditional European sense, but considered more like art directors. They created designs for the personas of the stars of the time. Head, who is considered one of the most influential costume designers in film history, won eight Oscars for her work, which included *Samson and Delilah* (1949) and *Roman Holiday* (1953).

styled by Patricia Field), but none quite as influential as the original *SATC*, which put nameplate necklaces, corsages, Fendi baguettes and Dior saddle bags on the universal map.

Experimenting

Since the turn of the millennium, SHOWstudio – a platform started by fashion photographer Nick Knight – has been exploring fashion films. Knight regularly collaborates with fashion designers to explore their work through moving images, and shows behind-the-scenes films. During the pandemic, fashion designers further explored the idea of fashion films over the in-person shows that had previously been the mainstay of the industry calendar out of necessity. While some critics argued it was not the same as going to a show and seeing the clothes in real life, there was something to be said for being able to step into the creative world of the designer beyond the pragmatism of a catwalk.

The condensed idea
Film is the new fashion runway

23 Streetwear

At the outset of her 2024 exhibition at the Fashion and Textile Museum in Bermondsey, London, legendary Biba designer Barbara Hulanicki is quoted as saying she started out wanting to make clothes for people on the street. While hers – gingham minidresses and languid Art Nouveau-inspired dresses – are not necessarily the archetypes we associate with streetwear today, her sentiment about them is relevant.

At its core, streetwear is as it sounds: what people wear on, and in, the street. Kim Jones, artistic director of Dior menswear, Fendi womenswear and couture, reiterated this when speaking to the style and streetwear publication *Highsnobiety* in 2019. He noted that, because people wear clothes on the street, everything is streetwear and essentially anything qualifies as such.

Streetwear is typically more affordable than designer brands (a lot of them are part-sportswear or part-performancewear labels) and its aesthetic is one that is overall more casual. Hoodies, sweatshirts, sneakers, graphic-print T-shirts and tracksuit bottoms are all considered streetwear. The genre captures grass-roots culture and subcultures, typically those associated with the worlds of hip-hop, skate, surf and graffiti, as opposed to the styles and fashions designers prescribe consumers to wear via the runway.

For example, during the 1990s, early hip-hop artists in New York – with whom streetwear is more contemporarily associated – rejected high fashion and instead wore sports clothing. This became a form of

Drops

Referring to the release of a new product arriving in store, 'drop' is a term used by streetwear brands. It indicates smaller, more exclusive, stock that devotees have to put time and effort into buying. Typically, there may only be a few set collections a year and, as in the case of Supreme, new product is released each Thursday. But when it's gone, it's gone.

streetwear, signifying a unique personal style, self-expression and identity. It also conveyed kudos. Streetwear has roots in all subcultures from the 1970s, through to the 1980s and 1990s. There is a nostalgic element to it.

Among trend theories is the idea that they trickle down; designers create collections that dictate the latest trends – hem lengths, colours, and so on – with a little help from magazines. But with streetwear, this is the other way round. It is the people's style and fashion nuances that influence the designers, and magazines write trend reports based on these (as in the case of London's 'youthquake').

Though streetwear remained a relatively niche interest to start with, over the last 15 years, the world of luxury and high fashion has sought to hijack it. Luxury brands need only to look at the queues forming outside outlets run by streetwear's key players, Supreme and Palace, in New York and London, respectively, where devoted and authentic fans queue for the 'drops', the rare pieces and the simple – but very cool – logo T-shirt.

In 2017, Louis Vuitton menswear, at the time headed up by Kim Jones, collaborated with Supreme. Better known for its trunks and handbags than its street-savoir-faire, Louis Vuitton is one of the world's most prestigious and storied luxury fashion houses. The collection featured a Louis Vuitton monogram canvas combined with the Supreme logo and received mixed reactions by press and fans (of both brands) alike. But it did cause plenty of hype, which is a key component of streetwear today.

Collaborations with artists often feature; the art world has long been entwined with streetwear culture because of its graffiti connections. Such has been the success of streetwear in recent years that both high fashion and mainstream fashion started to borrow from its template and terminology, including the introduction of 'drops'. The end goal? It creates hype.

Supreme, Palace, et al

The backdrop to all of this relies on a handful of brands. In 1994, American-British James Jebbia opened Supreme on Lafayette Street in New York, having previously worked with the surf/skate brand Stüssy. At Supreme, which now has 17 stores worldwide, he instigated a genius retail strategy, which built a cult following before becoming a global phenomenon. Producing limited editions, Supreme regularly collaborates with mainstream brands and artists for its stable of skating accessories and clothing, which as the mid-naughts progressed, attracted renewed interest.

The late Virgil Abloh launched his debut fashion brand Pyrex in 2012, reportedly taking deadstock Ralph Lauren flannel shirts and screen-printing them with the word 'Pyrex'. By 2013, he had established his highly influential Off-White brand, combining streetwear with art and luxury. He would succeed Kim Jones at Louis Vuitton.

It was also circa the early naughts, that the term 'normcore' started to circulate, a move towards more 'normal', or everyday, dressing. Jerry Seinfeld was a poster boy for the look. By 2014, the fashion brand Vetements had arrived on the scene and was inspired by 'real' clothes. It would go on to do collaborations with various sports brands, such as Reebok, to cement its place as a streetwear brand.

Givenchy, the Paris fashion house made famous by Audrey Hepburn, would also get itself a new creative director who boasted a streetwear style, Matthew Williams. His own label, 1017 ALYX 9SM, was known for its technical clips and subcultural twist on luxury.

Fashion's whole mood was changing. It wanted to be cool and authentic – something that Palace, arguably the UK's later counterpart to Supreme, had already been doing since 2009. Conceived by London skaters Lev Tanju and Gareth Skewis, who had been living in a squat reportedly ironically referred to as 'The Palace', Palace is known for its lo-fi aesthetic which borrows from the nostalgia of the 90s (rave culture, for example): tracksuits, shellsuits and windbreaker jackets. Known for its distinctive Penrose triangle logo the 'Tri-Ferg', designed by acclaimed illustrator Fergus Purcell, Palace first sold through skate shops and then began with pop-ups in various boutiques before opening stores that invited the same lengthy queues of dedicated fans as those at Supreme.

Skaters, punks, hip-hop heads – the young culture at large – all gravitated toward Supreme.
supreme.com

Hoodies became the garment to wear, fuelled also by the wunderkind designer Hedi Slimane, who has held roles at Dior Hommes, Saint Laurent and now Celine. In recent years, he has been inspired by youth culture and introduced hoodies in bright

Subculture

The term 'subculture' relates to a group of people within society who want to differentiate themselves from its accepted values and ideas. In a fashion context this translates as going against the trends and typical style expectations. Streetwear has championed an informal and sportswear-orientated way of dressing, making trophy items out of what were formerly day-to-day garments. Many fashion moments and movements have started by subcultures. Designers often look to to see what people are wearing on the 'street' for inspiration.

colours with the brand logo on them, and which typically sell for more than £700 each; *Dune* star Timothée Chalamet has been spotted wearing one.

Hypebeasts

Who would buy a hoodie like that? Perhaps a 'hypebeast', a term used to describe someone who likes to acquire fashionable clothes and shoes and is especially attracted to limited editions, such as trainers. The websites hypebeast.com and highsnobiety.com are squarely for this high-low streetwear-loving subculture. Hypebeast was established by Kevin Ma in 2005 as a sneaker blog and it went on to become a publicly listed media group in 2016. Highsnobiety also debuted in 2005, launched by David Fischer. Both platforms track emerging trends and limited-edition releases.

The condensed idea
Subculture style goes mainstream

24 The Internet

It is strange to think that, 25 years ago, the internet as we know it didn't exist – that no one was using it to buy weekly groceries or order deliveries, to book holidays or read the news. More importantly, for the purposes of this book, we were not using it buy clothes, read fashion gossip or to live-stream seasonal fashion collections.

The internet has brought a seismic shift to the way fashion is promoted and consumed. It has sped up the cycle of trends and, as a result, increased the production of fashion, both of which, it can be argued, have had a negative impact on the environment. But it has also meant that we are better informed about fashion than we have ever been before, both visually and informationally, and can access it on our phones and laptops wherever we are. We do not need to be a part of the fashion industry to see or enjoy it. The internet democratized fashion. A quarter-century on since the first fashion websites such as showstudio.com and vogue.com went live, we are now talking about digital fashion, avatars and skins. But it all really started with the idea of e-commerce.

e-commerce

Meaning 'electronic commerce', e-commerce has transformed the way we shop. At the click of a button, we can purchase a new holiday wardrobe, a top for tonight and a sale buy without having to go into a bricks-and-mortar store. It means that shopping can be done from the privacy of our homes or on the move.

Yet, despite the willingness with which we now routinely embrace this, it has not always been so. Customers were initially wary about giving credit card information to websites, and there was a general lack of consumer confidence. The worldwide web, which you could not use at the same time as a landline, was a scary new world, associated with dodgy chat rooms, pornography and slow dial-up that screeched like a fox. There was also an issue with returns. But as the technology improved, service got better and the luxe of a shop, and even the department store, was slowly replicated online.

Net-A-Porter, founded by the former *Vogue* fashion journalist Natalie Massenet, was established in 2000. Massenet managed to convince designer brands to stock their wares with her and suddenly, rather than sheepishly walking around the designer floor of a department store, or flicking through a monthly magazine, you could see – and buy – these clothes. NAP had no physical store. Neither did ASOS, which was also launched in 2000, catering to the other end of the spectrum. Clothes here, were fast fashion, replicas of what celebrities had been wearing at affordable prices. ASOS later expanded to stock high-street and other fashion brands.

Department stores and other brands slowly followed. Additional developments that contributed include the debut of PayPal, which was founded in 2000 and acquired by eBay in 2002, and Amazon, which began as a book-seller online in 1995 and began to sell clothing in 2002. Furthermore, e-com helped brands, especially emerging designers, showing that you did not have to do things the traditional way and have a store. The lack of changing-room facility was less than ideal, though. But, increasingly, technology has even been developed to remedy this using 3D body scanning. The internet was not the only way people shopped, however.

Street style

Disclaimer: I worked at vogue.co.uk from 2008–15, and one of my jobs was Street Chic, which meant taking pictures of people's style at events in London. It was street style. Something that took off big time as social media gained pace. Acclaimed fashion journalist Suzy Menkes wrote an article about it for *The New York Times' T* magazine

Show-going

Websites such as vogue.com, nowfashion.com, fashionnetwork.com and showstudio.com will publish images from a catwalk collection almost immediately after it has happened. They may well even live-stream it while it is on. This did not used to exist. Initially designers were wary of having their collections published on websites for fear of them being copied as collections are shown roughly six months before they appear in a store.

Front-row politics

At a fashion show, the front row is usually reserved for editors-in-chief, who run the magazines, and perhaps their fashion directors, as well as key buyers and celebrities. Over the past decade, the front row has been full of social media stars, bloggers and influencers, who have started to usurp the traditional editors.

in 2013, titled 'Circus of Fashion', in which she reflected on the peacockery of those standing outside the shows waiting to be chosen or ignored by photographers such as Scott Schuman (The Sartorialist) or Phil Oh. What they did was to help make stars out of an aspiring new type of non-traditional fashion journalist and promote personal style (no longer was it just about what was on the catwalk).

Social media

This is how many of the original influencers – they were called bloggers back then – began their careers in fashion. Social media was a brand-new type of platform requiring a brand-new type of content: bite-sized. Documenting their daily style choices on blogs and engaging with social media, these early influencers shared their insights with like-minded fans.

Facebook began in 2004, Twitter was created in 2006 and Instagram came along in 2010. The first Apple smartphone, the iPhone, was introduced in 2007. Social media enabled brands to take control of their own narrative and create their own content rather than rely on publications' coverage. It is the immediacy of social media that is the most important element. It took the viewer inside the shows, giving them trends and ideas months before they would usually have seen them in a supplement. Which is why the hierarchy of the fashion show front row began to change.

Influencers

Notable names from the early days include Tavi Gevinson, Bryanboy and Susie Bubble. Today, there are a hundred more. They gained a reputation for themselves commenting on fashion to a new audience that the magazines were not really targeting. (Most magazines did not work in tandem with their online counterparts and consisted of separate teams.) It was a grass-roots thing. As designers started to praise them for their fresh and innovative approach and saw potential collaborations in the pipeline, these names made their way up the fashion ranks – some of them even went on to work for major publications or became brands themselves.

As the name suggests, an influencer carries a certain amount of weight. It is to do with how many followers they have on Instagram or any other form of social media that a brand thinks is important. Often, they will be paid to create content, or collaborate with a brand to promote a new product. Posts that are adverts and have been paid for are required to note that on them.

The condensed idea
Transforming the way we experience fashion

25 Fast Fashion

Fast fashion has changed the ways in which fashion is both produced and consumed – and with great speed. Generally regarded as a new concept, it has ties to the emergence of brands such as the Spanish high-street retailer Zara, which was quick to get trend-led pieces in its stores in the late 1990s and early 2000s. Comparisons can be made to the 1960s emergence of a new and youth-orientated generation who wanted to differentiate themselves from their parents – a movement that coincided with the development of cheaper and more flexible fabric options.

The aim of fast fashion is to recreate catwalk ideas, or looks, for a fraction of the cost. Clothes are made for the masses and fast fashion is arguably the opposite of sustainable fashion for both production and consumption reasons. Names such as Primark, Forever 21 and H&M are considered fast-fashion brands, producing affordable, fashionable clothing and releasing new styles roughly every week.

Fast fashion is typically more reactive to real-time events – such as awards shows – or the discovery of a new trend on TikTok, and is bound up in the advance of technology. For example, social

Sweating

For all its glamour, and the joy and freedom it can bring, fashion and the clothing industry have a long-standing relationship with bad conditions for workers. Sweatshops, and the practice of sweating, were common during the 19th century. These were clothing manufacturers whose workers were paid low wages to work very long hours in poor conditions and they were widespread during the 1880s, when immigrants from eastern and southern Europe provided a burst of cheap labour across Europe and the United States. Conditions tended to be worse in large cities. By the middle of the 20th century, legislation had come in to control sweatshops, though the system was still in place in some countries in Asia.

media stirs consumer desire and fast turnaround capabilities enable production to fulfil that.

It was back during the Industrial Revolution, with the introduction of the sewing machine, that the pace of fashion was able to speed up. Suddenly it was available to more people, which meant there was more demand and prices started to drop.

According to the consulting firm McKinsey, from 2000–14 clothing production doubled and the number of garments purchased per capita increased by around 60 per cent, part of which it attributed to the rise of fast fashion. It is widely thought the fast fashion items are typically discarded after about seven wears. Indeed, Instagram has inadvertently prompted a wear-once generation of people who do not want to be photographed in the same thing twice. Where once there was just a handful of outlets, there are now many: Boohoo, ASOS and PrettyLittleThing in the United Kingdom, Fashion Nova in the United States, and Shein and Temu from China.

> The beauty of fashion should be accessible to everyone, not just the privileged few.
> Shein ethos

Shein and Temu

Shein, which claims to employ nearly 10,000 employees worldwide and sells to 150-plus countries, was formed in 2012 and offers what it describes as a wide range of options of design to fit moods and occasions. It is known for its vast quantities of clothes, for which it has come under fire (elle.com reported a figure of 9,000 items being uploaded to its website). There have also been allegations of copying and reports from fashion media of unethical treatment of workers.

Temu, meanwhile, launched in 2022 and became available in the United Kingdom, Spain, Italy, France and the Netherlands in 2023. Its success has been built on its low prices and discounts, as well as free shipping and returns. It also offers a wide range of products, but its quality and ethics have been called into question.

Cost cutting

Besides the environmental questions that fast fashion prompts (from the quality of the fabric to how many times it is worn before it ends up in landfill), it also raises questions over how garments are produced.

Disposable fashion

Fast fashion is often talked about as 'disposable fashion'. Largely produced to keep up with fluctuating trends so that consumers can update their wardrobes accordingly, an item can be in fashion one moment and out the other. This often makes an item of the wardrobe redundant, and therefore disposable, worn once, or perhaps not at all. Fast fashion is typically made from cheaper fabrics, those that require chemicals or plastic, and is sold at cheap prices. While this has brought a certain amount of democratization to fashion for fans wanting to get the latest look on a budget, it comes at an environmental cost.

If the end product is so cheap, what costs are being cut elsewhere? And who is suffering as a result? The production of fast fashion often relies on cheap labour and companies tend to turn to countries such as India, Bangladesh and Pakistan to find the workforces who make their products. Workers are often paid lower wages and sometimes operate in dangerous conditions.

On 24 April 2013, 1,134 people were killed and at least another 2,000 injured in the collapse of a factory building in Dhaka, Bangladesh. Clothing there, it was reported, was being made for international brands that included Primark, Bonmarché and Canada's Loblaw. The shocking incident brought attention to workers' rights and safety and cast a shadow over fast fashion. The owner of the building went to prison, but over a decade later campaigners say there is still work to be done to prevent such a disaster happening again.

Increasingly, high-street brands – widely considered fast-fashion culprits – have been stepping up their recycling, upcycling and sustainable initiatives as a way to counteract the production and consumption cycle of which they are a part.

Change

In March 2024, France's lower house of parliament approved a bill targeting fast fashion and ultra-fast fashion brands, such as Shein and

Boohoo. The idea is that they are subject to fees on fast-fashion products, are required to display an environmental score and are banned from advertising. The bill was praised by France's Ecological Transition Minister Christophe Béchu.

The condensed idea
Democratization of fashion versus the environment

26 The Flapper

The actress Louise Brooks, with her chiselled bob haircut, and Clara Bow, with her bee-stung lips, were the embodiment of the 'flapper', a term used to describe a new breed of free-spirited young woman in the 1920s.

Rejecting the societal expectations of what is was to be 'ladylike', and embracing instead a new-found sense of freedom that had come in the wake of World War I, the flapper cut her hair short, wore cloche hats, short skirts, strings of beads and T-bar shoes.

Prior to the flapper had been the Gibson Girl, circa 1890–1910. She wore a long skirt, wore a waist-cinching corset and piled her hair up onto her head. But the war saw women taking jobs that men would have had, which meant they gained an independence, both social and economic, that they had not previously enjoyed. Once the war ended, they did not want to give this up. The Gibson Girl ideal – though deemed a certain sort of independent and confident heroine in her day and one that did begin to bridge the gap between formerly restrictive dress and more active attire – started to lose her allure and no longer felt relevant.

In the 1900s the term 'flapper' had been used to describe a young debutante, according to some. Others thought it referred to youths who left their galoshes unbuckled, a noted trend. Now it became a leitmotif for the 1920s, a bohemian and modern era, in which many things started to change for women, and the flapper both signalled and embodied these. She was, it has been observed, one part stereotype – ubiquitous enough to be the subject of comics and illustrations – yet she also prompted a serious debate about feminism.

Women gained the vote in the United States in 1920; two years earlier those aged over 30 in Britain received it, too. Women were increasingly visible in society through sport, leisure activities and, importantly, work. They could drink and smoke, they could drive, and they abandoned female curves for boyish shapes. All of this movement called for an accompanying streamlined silhouette. There was a new awareness of the body in general, and the 1920s is noted as being the first time in history that women aspired to be thin. With the body-shaping corset largely not in use anymore (if they were, they were instead used to flatten curves), this came down to diet and exercise. Clothes were designed to show off the work that had gone into this.

The flapper notoriously danced the Charleston. At the time, the dance was considered indecent because of its flashy moves – in a 2014 article, the BBC compared it to twerking – notably the Charleston meant a woman could dance by herself as opposed to in the arms of a man. It was a taboo-breaking era.

For some people, all of this seemed resolutely indecent and inappropriate, irresponsible even, painting women as being self-absorbed and anti-feminist (though arguably the styles of dress without corsets, bustles and more would have been less time-consuming to put on). The flapper asserted independence and freedom for women, and instigated a discussion that would continue for the next 100 years. Besides conveying all of this by the way she acted, she also did so through her clothes.

> Uninhibited, full of high spirits, and determined to be famous, Scott wrote stories about such independent 'flapper' girls, Zelda modelled the dress and behaviours.
>
> Therese Anne Fowler, *The Telegraph*

The look

Deemed scandalous at the time, short dresses characterized the flapper look, straight in style and sleeveless, sometimes fringed, usually cut to the knee. To be a flapper was to be in style.

In 1925, F Scott Fitzgerald published *The Great Gatsby*, set in the infamous Jazz Age. His wife, Zelda Fitzgerald, is often referred to as being America's first flapper. That same year, hemlines began to rise above the knee, even shorter when they were cut into handkerchief points. Flappers wore make-up (which they happily applied in public), headbands, beads and pearls and attended events without chaperones. Designers Chanel, Vionnet, Schiaparelli, Lanvin and Patou are associated with the era's rule-breaking dressers – the bob haircut has been likened to Chanel's little black dress as being a fashion classic.

The bob

Throughout history, long hair has been associated with femininity. So, when a fashion for short hair arrived with the gamine look of the 1920s, it was provocative. It was at times severe – as in the Eton crop, which meant the back of the neck had to be shaved – and it was modern. Just as women's fashion was streamlining, so too did hairstyles. Louise Brooks helped to take the haircut mainstream as did the cloche hat – as part of the flapper look, it required a neat haircut to go with it. The cloche hat was designed by Caroline Reboux in 1908. Typically constructed from felted wool, it was moulded to the shape of the head, ideally mimicking the line of the bob haircut.

What was interesting about the flapper look was a simplicity that made it an ideal canvas for jewellery – bare arms for bangles, pieces styled following the Art Deco aesthetic of the time. Costume jewellery, as instigated by Chanel, became popular and acceptable. Feather boas and stoles adorned shoulders and necklines. Shoes also had more prominence – now seen, as hemlines no longer sought to hide them. Mary Jane shoes, a style that featured a strap across the instep, and T-bar styles became popular.

What did the men wear? Men's clothes were also becoming more informal as time went on and Oxford bags, a wide-legged style of trouser, were typically worn during the day, accompanied by slim-fitting blazers and perhaps a boater; at night, a tuxedo and cummerbund rather than a waistcoat. And while womenswear was becoming more masculine-infused – there was a vogue for 'la garçonne' – it would be a number of years still before women would start to fully share the components of a man's wardrobe.

> Zelda Fitzgerald, the southern belle turned jazz-age heroine, dubbed "the first American flapper" by her husband
> Sarah Hughes, *The Guardian*

Flapper trivia

According to vogue.com, the magazine ran a story called 'The Term "Flapper" Carries No Stigma' in 1917. Frances Marion released the film *The Flapper* in 1920, starring Olive Thomas, which charted Thomas as Ginger and her journey into living the flapper lifestyle. Other names often associated with the flapper era include the Missouri-born dancer Josephine Baker, recognized for her vibrant costumes, and Colleen Moore. An American actress, she also helped to popularize the bob haircut and appeared in silent motion pictures, as well as some talkies, or pictures with sound.

The condensed idea
A new type of feminism –
and freedom

27 Surrealists

I n fashion, the term 'surrealism' emerged in the 1920s and is most commonly associated with the fashion designer Elsa Schiaparelli, who became friends with prominent artists of the time, including Salvador Dalí, Jean Cocteau, Man Ray, Marcel Duchamp, Francis Picabia and the photographer Alfred Stieglitz.

As an art movement, one of the most important of the 20th century, it had originated between the two world wars and explored ideas concerning fantasy, dreams, the irrational and the unconscious mind, setting out to challenge the perceptions of the world. It had roots in another fashion movement, Dadaism, and the ideas and theories of Sigmund Freud, as well as literature. By the 1930s, surrealism had spilled into other fields besides art, specifically fashion and photography, which is where it has had a lasting impact on the industry, producing iconic designs and imagery that felt wholly ahead of their time, as well as unnerving, dramatic and, at times, kitsch.

Surrealist fashion imagery is often centred on the female body and, in particular, in obscuring parts of it to leave the mind wondering what it is seeing. German photographer Horst P Horst collaborated with Schiaparelli and Dalí – who is probably the most famous of the surrealist artists – and often created images in which the body was seen in isolation, contributing to a sense of erotica. Among his most famous images is one titled *Mainbocher Corset*, taken in 1939, which shows a woman wearing a corset from the back only, and in black and white. Overall, the effect turns her into something of an object.

Objects had the potential to take on new meanings in the world of surrealism, upending context with their displacement. Motifs often associated with the movement are lips, clocks and the use of trompe l'oeil. Schiaparelli was able to bring wit and charm to the surrealist field, pushing boundaries with her clothing and accessory designs – which, as per the surrealist philosophy, were not always what they seemed – while still affording them to be wearable. Where some of surrealism's artistic endeavours seemed charged and dangerous, she made it fun. Notably, the designer championed artistic collaborations, which today are a mainstay in fashion, especially for brands that want to show off their cultural kudos.

Elsa Schiaparelli

'Schiap' as she was called by friends, was described by Chanel – who was both her competition and her opposite – as an artist, as opposed to a fashion designer. The Italian creative, who hailed from Rome, had studied philosophy and married young, moving to New York. By the early 1920s, her husband had left her and she returned to Europe with her daughter, settling in Paris. It was there, at that point the creative centre of the world, home to authors and artists, thinkers and dancers, that Schiaparelli became involved in fashion. Her first design is noted as being a black jersey with a trompe l'oeil bow, which got noticed by a department store buyer who subsequently placed a large order with her. A first full collection debuted in 1929, Schiaparelli having opened a shop called Pour le Sport in the late 1920s.

Memorable designs of hers include a jacket made in collaboration with the artist Jean Cocteau in 1937, which featured an embroidered hand winding its way around the waist; the shoe hat created with Salvador Dalí, also in 1937, which saw a shoe perched upside down on the head with complete nonchalance, available with either a 'shocking pink' heel, or a black one; and the Lobster dress. The last is one of her best-known pieces because it was worn by Wallis Simpson. Another collaboration with Dalí, it took the lobster motif seen in works of his, such as the *Lobster Telephone* of 1936, and put it on a gown for the spring/summer 1937 couture collection. Deemed highly provocative, the pink shellfish printed on white organdie caused quite a stir when the duchess wore it.

Schiaparelli's designs were interesting, ironic and, later, iconic. She wanted to make things that attracted attention – buttons in the

Shocking pink

While Chanel is famed for her use of black, Schiaparelli introduced 'shocking pink' to the world. A bright magenta shade, it became quite the promotional tool for the brand. It was used on the box design for her perfume, Shocking, in 1937. Schiaparelli was a noted colourist and known to dye her zips the same colour as her fabrics to make even more of an impact.

From the French, meaning to 'deceive the eye', trompe l'oeil dates back to antiquity and was used to dramatic effect during the Renaissance period when artists were experimenting with perspective. The art technique has been borrowed by fashion – when a designer creates optical illusions to change the shape or overall perception of a garment, as Schiaparelli did with collars woven into sweaters. The effect can be achieved using various means of decoration or construction.

shape of acrobats diving down the front of a jacket, for example; hats in the shape of ice-cream cones. Further accessories played around with commonplace objects and included a compact that looked like a telephone dial and an 'aspirin' necklace. Quite brilliantly, and ahead of everyone, Schiaparelli created silk and cotton fabrics printed with her own press clippings for the opening of her new boutique in 1935 (during his tenure at Dior, the designer John Galliano famously put Dior newspaper prints on a bias-cut dress worn by Sarah Jessica Parker as Carrie Bradshaw in *Sex and the City*). And, as has been noted, by teaming up with artists, she managed to expand choices for women in a completely different way to her contemporary, Chanel.

Where Chanel broke the rules with uniformesque styles, Schiaparelli broke the rules with avant-garde looks that were outrageous, irreverent and hugely successful. Though the two were opposites, they worked in tandem when it came to their role in evolving and broadening the scope of what fashion could be, especially for women.

Other names that dabbled with surrealism included the French fashion house Rochas, who designed belt buckles in the form of miniature candelabras and crystal chandeliers. In 1938, the milliner Louise Bourbon produced a beret that mimicked an endive salad. By the end of the decade there was a whole host of mass-produced surrealist fashion items, including Dalí's clockface as a bag.

Surrealism revisited

It is possible to draw a comparison with surrealism and some of the fashions from the 1960s, many of which were also highly interlinked with artistic movements in the modern world. Fashion would become looser, less formal and more expressive in the post-war years, with surrealism being a favourite point of inspiration for many designers, especially alongside the rise of technology.

For the spring/summer 2011 season, the Greek designer Mary Katrantzou created a headline-grabbing collection with lampshade skirts beneath *World of Interiors* vistas in digital prints that had 3D depth. The Central Saint Martins' alumnus had previously graduated with a collection inspired directly by perfume bottles.

Italian fashion house Moschino has often played around with cultural motifs, showcasing dresses as grandfather clocks, items of furniture, jackets with cutlery for fastenings, tray bustiers, chandelier headdresses and sending rubber rings down the catwalk as accessories.

And ever since his appointment at Loewe, Jonathan Anderson has pushed a surreal art narrative at the Spanish heritage house. Shoes have been trapped in dresses, giant lips have stood in for busts, balloons have made for shoes and decoration on dresses, rose stems have formed the heels on shoes – he has taken it mainstream.

Daniel Roseberry, installed as creative director at Schiaparelli in 2019, continues to champion the legacy of Elsa. A gem-studded robot baby (not real) was carried out at a recent couture collection, while his often bejewelled optical illusions are also popular on the red carpet.

The condensed idea
Bringing fantasy to fashion

28 The New Look

The year was 1947, the date was 12 February, and the look was new: Dior's New Look, christened by the then editor of *Harper's Bazaar*, Carmel Snow. She had observed that Christian Dior designs – nipped-in waists with splaying skirts and full hips, a pointed, pronounced bust and round shoulders – had quite a new look to them.

It was the antithesis of government-mandated wartime frugality and masculine uniforms that had come before. Dior would instead dress the female body in lovely fabrics and luxurious finery – what he had described as 'flower women'. Rationing be gone.

Paul Poiret and Coco Chanel had not long created a modern-day and freeing wardrobe for women, one of easy-chic but practical lines that had been cemented by the pragmatic requirements of wartime. But now hemlines dropped 23cm (9in) and wasp-waist corsets and petticoats spilling from the waist were back in fashion, thanks to Mr Dior. For some, this seemed like a backward move. Glamorous and optimistic on the one hand, it could also be seen as frivolous with all that fabric (up to 13.5m/45ft according to some sources). It was also a throwback to a pre-war era, and a controlled and compromised way of dressing.

Harper's Bazaar published a series of sketches that detailed the construction of the look, taken from Dior's Corolle line, a botanical term that references the petals of a flower, or open petals. The silhouette consisted of padding over the bust and hips (the familiar Dior Bar jacket is part of the New Look), as well as whalebone and wire to construct the waist. Yards of material were used, with tulle added to emphasize the shape.

Featuring rounded shoulders, a cinched waist, and very full skirt, the New Look celebrated ultra-femininity and opulence in women's fashion.

Metropolitan Museum of Art, New York

Other designers, it has been noted, had already been working towards similar silhouettes as early as 1939, but their efforts had been interrupted by the Second World War. Meanwhile, American *Vogue* had proffered the hourglass figure that same year and the waist cincher, or *guêpière*, was around from 1945.

Recognition

Dior received the French Legion of Honour award for his role in the fashion and textile industry in 1950. That same year, he presented a collection in London to Queen Elizabeth II and Princess Margaret.

The New Look signified a return to glamour and it came from the mind of a designer whose name went on to become one of the best-known in fashion, both historically and contemporaneously. Today it is part of the Louis Vuitton Moet Hennessy (LVMH) luxury conglomerate founded by Bernard Arnault, and Italian fashion designer Maria Grazia Chiuri, formerly of Valentino, is its first solo female creative director; she often draws on Dior's New Look, combining elements of it with themes of female empowerment, for her collections. There have been eight creative directors besides Dior himself, including a co-directorship: Yves Saint Laurent, Marc Bohan, Gianfranco Ferré, John Galliano, Bill Gaytten, Raf Simons, an interim Lucie Meier with Serge Ruffieux, then Maria Grazia Chiuri. Kim Jones leads the menswear and follows in the footsteps of Kris Van Assche and Hedi Slimane.

Christian Dior

Monsieur Dior was born on 21 January 1905, in Granville, France, to an industrialist father, Maurice, and a housewife mother, Madeleine Martine. She was known for her elegant outfits and taste in decor and lifestyle, which rubbed off on her five children, Christian especially. The family moved to Paris, where Christian studied at L'École Libre des Sciences Politiques, in the early 1920s. However, Dior's interests lay in the arts, architecture, music, drawing and painting.

His family lost its fortune during the Great Depression, after which Christian learned fashion drawing, selling designs to magazines as well as couturiers such as Jean Patou, Nina Ricci, Maggy Rouff and Balenciaga. Dior went on to join Lucien Lelong's design team in 1941 and by 1945 had met Marcel Boussac, who aided him in creating his own fashion house.

Surprisingly, Dior's career spanned only 22 collections; he died in 1957. Yet his name has been cemented in the history books forever and his idea behind the New Look is a lasting legacy, a much referenced moment in fashion. Notably, the business grossed $15 million annually and employed 1,500 people, accounting for 55 per cent of all Paris couture exports by 1953, according to *WWD*. In 1957, Dior's global reputation was such that he featured on the cover of *Time* magazine.

Dior's idea was to relieve women of the drudgeries of wartime and enhance femininity and beauty. The house was initially financed by Marcel Boussac and drew on romance and nostalgia, which helped put Paris once again at the heart of the global fashion scene.

Opposition

During wartime, a sober approach to dressing had become the norm. The corset had quite long fallen out of favour, a symbol of the past, and women were now engaged in new sectors of society in a way they had not been before. So, while the New Look brought with it a lost femininity, it also brought controversy. English tailors were said to protest against the length of Dior's skirts. In 1947, during a visit to the United States, the designer encountered the hostile banners of the Little Below the Knee Club, whose members were unimpressed by the reintroduction of these longer lengths and impractical skirts. But by 1948, the New Look was winning people over and it would continue to be popular throughout the 1950s. A decade later, Dior's successor, the young Yves Saint Laurent, would propose the trapeze silhouette, an opposite once again.

The new New Look? Balenciaga

While Christian Dior popularized a svelte silhouette that nipped and tucked to pre-wartime glamour standards, fashions would soon change again. A contemporary of his, the Spanish designer Cristóbal

Balenciaga, had already earned himself a reputation as a leading couturier by the early 1930s, moving to Paris later in the decade. His impactful designs were often formal: gowns that took on striking shapes, billowing backs, tiered forms, bulbous skirts, cocoon-like and sculptural. He was known as a master of shape and volume, which would be shown off to the best effect with his talent also for colour. Among his noted new silhouettes were the 'barrel' style and the sack dress; he also explored trapeze lines on dresses.

The condensed idea
Looking forwards or backwards?

29 Americana

The trade title *Women's Wear Daily* (*WWD*) declared that, for spring/summer 2023, among menswear, Americana was one of the most in-demand trends of the season. What it meant by that was the iconography, motifs and themes generally associated with the cultural heritage of America. Just like the size of the country itself, those talking points are varied and expansive – in fashion terms, they are most often attributed to things like the college prep look, Western cowboys, surfer/skater styles from 1970s California, and the grunge scene from Seattle.

For the spring/summer 2016 season, the American designer Marc Jacobs plundered the world of red, white and blue for what felt like a streamer-filled collection or a walking version of July 4. Hedi Slimane, appointed creative director at French fashion house Celine in 2018, often explores American youth culture for his collections. And since British designer Stuart Vevers took over Coach, the New York-based fashion brand formed in 1941, he has leaned into nostalgic Americana spirit for varsity jackets and prairie dresses. Contemporary fashion has long had an obsession with Americana, no doubt because it has so many facets.

The Ivy League look

More generally known as preppy style, the Ivy League look took inspiration from the elite prep schools of the United States' East Coast, such as Harvard, Yale, Dartmouth and Princeton, where social attire conveyed political and economic status. These colleges, in turn, stemmed from British public schools such as Harrow and Charterhouse, where straw boaters and 'house' colours were uniform staples.

The look was built around a blazer, a button-down shirt, a rep stripe tie (featuring diagonal stripes and a mainstay of private schools and clubs), flat-fronted trousers, loafers and/or lace-ups. Correct footwear was considered very important. A more casual look might include a Shetland or Fair Isle knit – the type made popular by Edward, Prince of Wales, during the 1920s. Part of the wider uniform included cotton polo shirts with cap sleeves, top-sider deck shoes, the letterman sweater and the varsity jacket.

Origins

World War II had a huge impact on clothes, getting dressed and fashion – and not only as far as women's status was concerned. Teenagers, a growing market, also wanted to cultivate their own identity, no longer wanting to dress like their parents. The preppy style, however, was not as extreme or rebellious as that of other styles that were emerging around the same time, such as the beatnik or the rockabilly. Indeed, it had been constructed to be this way, and part of its genius was its ability to look casual and carefree at the same time.

For women, the 'bobbysoxer' look was popular from the mid-1940s, made up of knee-length skirts and penny loafers. Short-sleeved cardigans and sweaters with Peter Pan collars beneath, as well as skirts stiffened with petticoats featuring motifs such as poodles and musical notes, were also key. Prom dresses, first recollected in 1894 at a college in Massachusetts, were worn during the 1950s, as part of the American high-school graduation ritual. As seen on screen – *Happy Days*, on air from 1974–78, and the film *Grease*, released in 1978, recalled the nostalgia for this kind of 1950s Americana.

The look was both smart and casual, arising from the Ivy Leaguer's need to wear items suitable for both sporting and social occasions. Notably, there were rules about what was and was not acceptable, which gave it an insider feel and sense of exclusivity. The varsity jacket is seen as particularly embodying the nature of the look: relaxed while displaying a sense of achievement.

As fodder for fashion trends, these secret codes, layers and nuances do not necessarily matter as much anymore but the look's ability to be smart-casual chimes in a modern world that has become increasingly less formal.

Designers

Ralph Lauren and Tommy Hilfiger are names linked to Americana. Both US designers, they have celebrated the hallmarks of the country's clothes with collections that have further cemented these styles as

American classics and sold them as part of the American dream, which is closely associated with success and upward mobility.

Among other things, Lauren is famous for introducing the 'prairie look', which has been a hallmark of the brand ever since the end of the 1970s. Aesthetically, it is very American frontier in feel. Born Ralph Lipschitz, he worked at Brooks Brothers (who dressed Ivy Leaguers) in New York and later, in 1967, joined Beau Brummell Ties. Ties are really where it all started. He debuted a collection of them before he did a full menswear collection. In the early 1970s, he opened a Polo by Ralph Lauren store in Bloomingdales and soon a Ralph Lauren standalone store. The Polo line is sportier than the classic Ralph Lauren line, but both tap into building a strong sense of American style – sportswear, casualwear, smartwear that is neat and crisp, but not confrontational. It is classic and elegant, and exudes that smart-casual of Ivy League style, appropriate for any occasion.

> Reflecting a distinctive American perspective, we have been an innovator in aspirational lifestyle branding and believe that, under the direction of internationally renowned designer Ralph Lauren, we have had a considerable influence on the way people dress and the way that fashion is advertised and celebrated throughout the world.
> ralphlauren.co.uk

Icons

America's most famous fashion icons include Jackie Kennedy, Grace Kelly, James Dean, Brooke Shields (for Calvin Klein), and a great many more who inhabit the various style semantics of what makes Americana. In 2021, The Costume Institute explored this theme with the exhibition In America: A Lexicon of Fashion, which looked at eight decades of clothing through fashion, from the established designers who helped to build it, to the new names of the future who are shaping it.

Tommy Hilfiger, similarly, took this blend of preppy style as a basis for his own brand, a menswear line that started in 1985. The brand describes itself as a pioneer of American style, one that adds to that with a modern twist. It is perhaps no surprise that US fashion is known for its wearability and commerciality – it was at one point the hub of ready-to-wear. Pertinently, Hilfiger often draws on the red, white and blue colour palette of the American flag, which it fuses with sportswear and denim – hardwearing and durable, denim itself has roots in the American West, again a talking point of Americana style.

Americana fashion today

The very broad and varied nature of the United States means that neat preppy types are as much a representation of Americana fashion as country-and-western checks, cowboy boots and Stetsons. More recently, brands such as Gap, Banana Republic and Abercrombie & Fitch have represented modern America more in line with this type of preppy fashion; while the American West from time to time swings round as a main fashion trend, with catwalks full of pie-crust collars, petticoat skirts and prairie dresses, yolked shirts, chaps and fringed jackets. Louis Vuitton's Pharrell Williams made it the inspiration for his menswear autumn/winter 2024 collection, and shortly afterwards Beyoncé released her album, titled *Cowboy Carter*. Suddenly, the American West was back in fashion.

The condensed idea
Selling the American dream through clothes

30 Space Age

I n 1961, two significant events took place that brought the world of space and fashion together: Soviet cosmonaut Yuri Gagarin became the first man in space and André Courrèges, the French fashion designer, opened his Paris fashion house.

During the early 1960s, television became widely available, making footage of astronauts accessible to many. France had also declared it would be joining the space race in a post-war period that saw competition between the East and the West in the field of science and innovation. In 1957, the Soviet satellite Sputnik successfully launched into orbit, bringing a mix of hope and fear about the future, while the US announced a programme of space research, and in 1969, Neil Armstrong and Buzz Aldrin landed on the moon in Apollo 11.

The decade, book-ended with firsts, had been foregrounded by predictions in the 1950s about how we might live in the future. In both decades, new fabrics and technical fibres were emerging in everyday wear, sometimes as by-products of chemical research that had been undertaken for military, aeronautical and space purposes. Crease-resistant and quick-drying, synthetics enabled the rise of affordable clothing, attracting a younger, modern audience. Designers, too, were able to explore the different aesthetic and structural properties of these new materials. Manufacturers, meanwhile, were looking for alternatives to cotton and wool. Technology flourished at this time, and the competition between the East and West is what made the space age a reality; so, too, did a space-age style for those who had no intention of leaving planet Earth.

Space-age style

Space exploration inspired a new wave of utopian thinking about the future, and by the mid-1960s, it had become a fashion look largely defined by body stockings, jumpsuits, unitards, leggings, tunics, coats and minidresses accessorized with sequins, go-go boots, moon boots, wide belts, helmets and visors. Colours were bold and geometric. Fabrics were often stiff and held their own shape rather than draping the body. Clothes made from PVC, vinyl and plastic became an interesting proposition, while Velcro and zips were used as fastenings.

On film

Barbarella and *2001: A Space Odyssey*, both released in 1968, are two films that embody the space-age style, showing in visual terms how much it shaped culture at the time. Paco Rabanne is credited with designing one, or some, of the costumes for Jane Fonda in *Barbarella*, while British fashion designer Hardy Amies designed the space-age flight attendants' tailoring in *2001: A Space Odyssey*.

It is not that the space-age trend rejected traditional fabrics, but it did emphasize the man-made, particularly plastic.

Lines were clean and utilitarian. Inbuilt in the style were military connotations – perhaps not surprising given that the 1960s was not the first time the future, or rather the idea of it, was in fashion. Futurism had also been a hallmark of 1930s design. Garments of the 1960s future were often unisex, designed to function and therefore devoid of any real decoration.

The collections of Pierre Cardin, one of a trio of significant fashion designers during the space-age era, reportedly were shown by models en masse, as if they were indeed the crew of a spaceship. Cardin was part of a group of Paris-based designers who were utilizing the latest high-tech synthetic sports fabrics to create their space-age world.

Three designers

It is André Courrèges who is considered the author of the space-age look, according to some, his name uttered alongside those of Pierre Cardin and Paco Rabanne. He was inspired by architecture and modernist forms and apparently said there was much in common between designing a building and making a dress. He launched the Moon Girl collection in 1964, which was white and silver and featured trousers with matching tunics and thigh-high minidresses. Precisely cut, his designs featured few curves and were widely copied.

Meanwhile, Cardin was a conceptual designer, a pioneer also of the mini-skirt and of unisex dressing. He combined fashion and science for his landmark Cosmo Corps collection of 1964, which featured white knitted all-in-ones worn beneath tabbards and tubular dresses among its creations for men and women. Pinafore dresses and tunics in bright colours with stylized cut-outs and worn with PVC high boots made for more commercial versions later on.

Paco Rabanne was known for his chain-mail minidresses and body coverings made from metal discs, having initially made a name for himself with his plastic jewellery. The Spanish designer brought his experience in architecture and industrial design to his first body jewellery collection in 1966, titled 'Twelve Unwearable Dresses in Contemporary Materials' and presented at Hotel George V in Paris. The sheaths were constructed from striking squares and discs of rhodoid, a cellulose acetate plastic, and attached to fabric underneath. Rabanne, who Chanel apparently described as a metal worker, was also a pioneer of recycling materials and experimented with hammered steel, aluminium jersey and paper for dresses.

With the work of these three men fashion became modern, industrial and innovative, charting brand new waters at a time when the world was gearing itself towards youth.

Different perspectives

Op art, a term that originated in 1964 to describe art that explores optical effects that trick the eye, was starting to filter into fashion at the same time. It included Yves Saint Laurent's famous Mondrian dress. Designers simplified op art into bold patterns and shapes, which felt modern and, in many ways, as futuristic – and optimistic – as those of their space-age counterparts.

Fashion historians have noted that a key part of futuristic fashion was the idea of clothing as uniform, which suggested order, but also glamorous forms of travel. Emilio Pucci, the Italian brand known for its geometric prints and patterns, designed the flight attendant uniforms for the American airline Braniff in 1965, as part of a company makeover. Apparently, they even came with 'space bubble' helmets to protect hairstyles when airside, but these were soon dropped owing to their impracticality.

Looking to the future

Fashion's relationship with the future today is one based largely on implementing sustainable and circular practice and avoiding the

Not forgetting

French designer Emanuel Ungaro worked with Courrèges from 1964–65, before establishing his own house with textile artist Sonja Knapp. His first collections, it is noted, followed the futuristic lines of Courrèges but in stronger, brighter colours. Meanwhile, Rudi Gernreich explored the use of clear vinyl and plastic – he is deemed the US counterpoint to Paris' space-age trio, playing with different materials and cut-outs, especially with swimwear, and challenging what the future of fashion could look like. And the UK's Mary Quant can also be considered part of this movement; she brought her primary brights to the look, in short, simple shapes.

plastics and synthetics that were standard for the space-age movement. Nevertheless, designers continue to think about what clothes will look like years from now, resulting a kind of retro-futurism with medieval-meets-techno styles and fabrications along the lines of those by Nicolas Ghesquière at Louis Vuitton for spring/summer 2018, which saw frock coats paired with sneakers and silver trousers. The French designer is well known for his future-facing styles, sometimes bordering on science fiction. During his Balenciaga tenure, he pushed the boundaries about how sci-fi fashion could be.

The intriguing thing about the original space-age clothing is how, at the time, it felt and looked incredibly futuristic, yet today it is dated – a hallmark of the 1960s era.

The condensed idea
New futuristic styles and material exploration

31 Youthquake

It was *Vogue* editor Diana Vreeland who coined the term 'youthquake' in 1965, to describe the vibrant, exciting and – pertinently – youthful scene that was bursting out of London. It remains in fashion history as one of the most groundbreaking times to be alive – The Beatles, the Rolling Stones, the mini-skirt, go-go boots, dark eyeliner and pale pink lips, Vidal Sassoon sculpted bob haircuts, reprised dandy looks, mods and rockers, op art and pop art. A year later, *Time* magazine described the British capital as the 'Swinging City'. London was home to a revolution in culture, style and music, all colliding to intoxicating effect.

> But it was Vreeland – at the helm at *Vogue* from 1962 to 1971 – who initially noticed this shake up in 'Swinging London', when young people were adopting everything from Beatlemania to the mini-skirt. This was, after all, the age of the British Invasion.
>
> Hilary Weaver, *Vanity Fair*

After World War II, British teenagers found they had more disposable income than their parents had had when they were teenagers. They were part of a first generation who were able to experience expanded opportunities in everything from education to leisure pursuits. They channelled this spending power into music and fashion. No longer did they want to dress like their parents or kowtow to the adult formalities of a former era. Societal expectations, particularly for women, did not feel relevant anymore. Fashion was becoming increasingly unisex and men and women could shop at the same stores. Britain's youth culture burgeoned under these new baby boomers.

Tights

The journalist and author Brigid Keenan, who held the job of young fashion editor at the *Sunday Times* during the 1960s, told *Glamour* magazine in 2016 that tights were incredibly important at the time. She said they provided liberation and that they made mini-skirts, an emblem of the era, possible.

The seeds towards freedom in dress had already been planted during the war as women took on men's jobs and their roles in society. And while the New Look of 1947 had impressed at the time, perceived as groundbreaking in the face of austerity, its restrictive construction and ideal of pre-war femininity did not appeal to a new generation keen to embrace what life had to offer. It became an icon of the past.

Material dreams

The youthquake era was also one of new synthetic fabrics and man-made materials, which offered up fun and exciting possibilities to designers, manufacturers and consumers alike. Plastic, Perspex, PVC, polyester, acrylic, nylon, rayon, Spandex, and even paper, made fashion fun. It was also becoming disposable.

A retail boom saw the debut of the boutique (regarded as a British invention), which catered for this new generation. Mary Quant's Bazaar fashion boutique on King's Road, London, captured the spirit of the times. It opened in 1955 and soon became known for its 'Chelsea Look', silhouettes that allowed movement, that had a childlike charm in their simple shapes and bright colours. Pinafore dresses and mini-skirts – among the most revolutionary designs of the time – and modern, future-facing ideas.

It was not the only hot spot of the time. Carnaby Street, once upon a time a rundown back street in Soho, became ripe for studio space for fashion students Marion Foale and Sally Tuffin, who went there, to Marlborough Court, in the early 1960s, opening a shop in 1964. The pair had met while studying at the Royal College of Art, and had apparently graduated with the shared determination that they would not go the conventional route of completing an apprenticeship, but instead decided to set up their own business.

They made informal dresses in bright prints and loud colours, that were young, fun and in the spirit of the age. The duo featured in British *Vogue*'s 'Young Ideas' column, headed up by the fashion journalist Marit Allen. They also popularized the womenswear suit, making it unabashedly seductive. Allen would have no shortage of other designers to fill her page, for London was booming and word was spreading fast, to the United States, of course famously to Vreeland.

Barbara Hulanicki opened her first Biba boutique on Abingdon Road in Kensington in 1964. Tommy Roberts opened Kleptomania in

Kingly Street, just behind Carnaby Street, in 1966. It was suddenly all about Carnaby Street and Knightsbridge, the cool places to be, away from the traditional Bond Street and Savile Row. These new haunts, and the boutiques that filled them, provided a place for self-expression, which was the coolest currency of all.

Icons

Besides the boutiques, and London itself, key names to have come out of the youthquake – or rather to have defined it – were models Twiggy and Jean Shrimpton and the photographer David Bailey.

> **The Beatles didn't make the Swinging Sixties, the Swinging Sixties made the Beatles.**
> David Bailey

Twiggy was named so because she was very thin. Her boyish figure, eye-linered eyes and short crop embodied a gamine look that was now accepted in society. She became an icon and would appear on the cover of *Vogue*. Bailey, in turn, captured the swinging scene on pages inside the magazine.

What was significant about London's youthquake and the Swinging Sixties is that it was youth culture and what people were wearing on the streets – often made by a bunch of recently graduated art students – that inspired *Vogue* to report on it and create columns to capture it. Trends up until this point had been dictated by the designers or by the magazines. Here, it was the reverse, and the ideas on the street were bubbling up to those above.

Word of the year

In a surprising twist to the timeline of the term 'youthquake', it became the *Oxford English Dictionary*'s word of the year in 2017, some five decades after it first appeared. It should be noted that it was not the word of the year according to other dictionaries/outlets, but had apparently experienced an increase in usage to make it top their list.

The end

British fashion historian James Laver points out that the 1960s can be divided into two distinct periods, 1960–67, what is commonly thought of as being the Swinging Sixties, and thereafter, 1968, when he points out the master couturier Balenciaga – the acclaimed Spanish designer known for his volume, shape and innovation – retired. So too, it seemed, had the optimism. Politics and the economy took over, as did the hippy movement – loose shapes, free love, peace and tie-dye – a counter-culture style that had emerged during 1960s, primarily in the United States.

The condensed idea
Social revolution through style

32 Punk

Anarchic and out to shock, the punk movement originated in London, England, during the 1970s – some pinpoint the exact timeline as summer 1975 to January 1978. It also has American roots in New York, specifically the Lower East Side and the club CBGB, founded in 1973 by Hilly Kristal, and bands like the New York Dolls.

At punk's heart was a protest against the establishment. An urban movement, in the United Kingdom it is associated with disenchanted teenagers who were largely unemployed and who set out to intimidate, blaspheme and subvert with in-your-face and daring attitudes and a style that often bordered on the indecent – for a time, at least.

The movement was heavily bound up in music, fashion and politics – expressing the latter through the former – and can be traced back to one particular street in west London, King's Road, and the fashion design duo of Vivienne Westwood and Malcolm McLaren. Arguably, they are punk's best-known protagonists, though not the only ones.

Westwood and McLaren

The late Vivienne Westwood, who later in life was an activist and environmentalist, was a self-taught designer; her story is as punk as the movement itself. She grew up in Glossop, Derbyshire, and in the

The punk look

Punk encouraged a DIY approach to dressing, which in part empowered the wearer to construct their own identity. It was about self-expression as well as shock factor and was a look for both sexes. Black leather jackets, torn trousers, ripped T-shirts featuring provocative slogans or vulgar messages, string vests, dog chains worn around the neck, mohair sweaters, clompy Doc Marten boots, safety pins and studs on clothes and as piercings on the body, brightly coloured dyed hair, sometimes fashioned into spikes, are all classic hallmarks of punk style.

1960s she met Malcolm McLaren, an art student, with whom she would open a cult shop at 430 King's Road. Politically, McLaren was interested in the French Situationists who wanted to eradicate capitalism, and this thinking would have an impact on Westwood.

From 430 King's Road, the pair masterminded a new type of fashion that came to epitomize this youthful sense of unrest. In accordance with punk's DIY approach, Westwood could be found making up garments herself at her Thurleigh Court home in Balham. Later 430 King's Road became the destination for punks: a place where rules were broken and new ways of making fashion were born.

The pair had taken a trip to the United States in the early 1970s, and while there, had been inspired by the rumblings of American punk in bands like The Ramones and New York Dolls. McLaren went on to manage the latter for a time before bringing together his own anarchic band of punk ambassadors, the Sex Pistols, from 1975–78.

430 King's Road

The name of the shop changed depending on the theme of its collections, but throughout the decade all of these iterations encompassed the ideology of punk and were stylistically deviant. When the shop first opened, in 1971, it was called Let It Rock; a year later was renamed Too Fast To Live, Too Young To Die. It was in this iteration that clothes focused on customized T-shirts with printed graphics and slogans, including the word 'rock' spelled out in boiled chicken bones.

It was renamed Sex in 1974 and the name was spelled out in big rubberized letters. Their shop assistant at the time, Pamela Rooke aka Jordan, became a punk pin-up, dressing in bondage and fetishistic garments in the store and apparently causing outrage on her commute to work on the train. In 1976, the shop became Seditionaries, and Westwood experimented with straps and zips, motorcycle leathers, torn-looking dresses, chains and studs – members of the Sex Pistols would wear various looks from this era, cementing the designer's status as the high priestess of punk.

> I did not see myself as a fashion designer but as someone who wished to confront the rotten status quo through the way I dressed and dressed others
>
> Vivienne Westwood, *Vivienne Westwood*

Sex Pistols

Ambassadors for the movement, the Sex Pistols band was made up of Johnny Rotten, Paul Cook, Steve Jones, Glen Matlock and, later, Sid Vicious, all of whom would become known for songs like 'Anarchy in the UK' and 'God Save The Queen', an anthem that they were often banned from playing. Their anti-establishment songs were matched by raucous behaviour that got them into trouble, which was very punk, after all.

The Victoria and Albert Museum, in London, has several Vivienne Westwood items among its collections, an ensemble from the Seditionaries era often on show in its fashion section. In 2013, The Metropolitan Museum of Art, in New York, put on the exhibition Punk: Chaos to Couture, which took a closer look at the impact of the movement on high fashion and featured around 100 designs for men and women, including original punk garments, as well as more recent iterations. The idea was to explore how the worlds of haute couture and ready-to-wear had actually borrowed visual codes from punk, and to look at the relationship between the former's 'made to measure' and the latter's 'do it yourself'.

Legacy

Punk's impact was not confined to street style, but was seen on catwalks during the 1980s and 1990s, and even into the 21st century. Notable designers who have played around with punk over the years include Junya Watanabe, Matty Bovan, Charles Jeffrey, Comme des Garcons, Alexander McQueen, John Galliano and Jean Paul Gaultier.

In the wake of punk came various subculture spin-offs such as cyberpunk, a combination of punk style with a futuristic and technological element woven in. Leather, PVC, rubber and accessories made from circuit boards completed the look. Goth, arguably a more macabre and darkened version of punk, enjoys some crossovers with punk in terms of fashion, but is ultimately more engrossed with Victorian and Edwardian styles and comes laced with a sense of mystery and magic.

Westwood passed away in December in 2022. While her career was expansive, traversing the worlds of history and activism for her designs at different stages of her life, she will forever be known for her role in the iconic punk movement. Regardless of how her aesthetics might have changed, there was always something punk aka rebellious about Westwood, in her spirit and her designs, until the end.

The condensed idea
An anti-establishment rebellion expressed through music and fashion

33 Studio 54

An image comes to mind when thinking about Studio 54: Bianca Jagger on a white horse, making quite an entrance to the famed New York club which, despite its long-lasting and glamorous reputation, was open for just three years.

The actress, and then wife of Mick Jagger, has since set the record straight that she did not ride the horse into the club, but the legend, like so many things associated with Studio 54, endures. This is especially true of the fashion: the glamour, the glitter, the disco, the celebrity, the exclusivity. It was here that Hollywood hung out with fashion designers and fashion designers became celebrities.

Disco-ball and dance-floor-ready ensembles set a new agenda, embodying a hedonistic and decadent attitude towards life. They were the work, typically, of Roy Halston, Diane von Furstenberg, Calvin Klein, Stephen Burrows, Norma Kamali, Stephen Sprouse and the jeweller, Elsa Peretti, all of whom became household names as a result.

Studio 54 ran from 1977–80 on West 54th Street in Midtown, Manhattan, and is among the most famous clubs to have played a role in fame, fortune and fashion. Opened by Ian Schrager and Steve Rubell, it had a strict door policy. Inside would be the great minds of

Fashion fever

While glam rock was taking off in the United Kingdom in the 1970s, an equal smattering of sequins but a little less androgyny and flamboyance was emerging in the United States. It marked a move towards disco, which went mainstream thanks to the 1977 John Travolta-starring film *Saturday Night Fever* and the accompanying Bee Gees soundtrack, 'Staying Alive'. The actor's white three-piece suit with its exaggerated lapels helped to promote disco style (and fetched $260,000 at auction in 2023). The suit was made from polyester, a synthetic stretch fabric that lent itself easily to groovy moves.

the time – artists Andy Warhol (famous for his own Factory enterprise) and Jean-Michel Basquiat, actress Anjelica Huston and, of course, Jagger – who would often be dressed by Roy Halston, a designer known for his fluid eveningwear and silk kaftans, or halter neck jumpsuits.

Such was its allure and lasting legacy that designers to this day reference the club as inspiration for their collections. Marc Jacobs' spring/summer 2011 felt like it was an ode to the moment: his show saw models with vivid 1970s make-up, blooms in their crimped hair, big floppy hats and halterneck dresses, some billowing, some sensuous. Collections from Tom Ford also have a whiff of the club's 1970s decadence. In fashion speak, uttering Studio 54 sums up both a mood and an era – one that brought us Diane von Furstenberg's 'wrap dress', a wraparound style that has become a wardrobe classic, Stephen Burrows' flirty hemlines and Norma Kamali's high-shine outfits.

Halston

Roy Halston epitomized a new type of modern dressing in the 1970s, offering wearable and modern pieces and versatile separates. The idea of one-stop dressing and wardrobe staples came into play. Halston, who hailed from Iowa, attended the University of Indiana and the Chicago Institute. Like many designers, his entry into the industry was through hats. He opened a millinery salon in a Chicago hotel in 1953 and designed a great many hats for Jackie Kennedy, including the much copied felt pillbox design. In 1966, he began to do ready-to-wear and showed his first collection in 1968. Clients of his included Gloria Swanson, Liza Minnelli and Deborah Kerr. His long, slinky dresses and tie-dyed chiffon featured among a fairly extensive repertoire that was favoured by American socialites. And he was a regular sighting at Studio, as it was known.

DVF

Diane von Furstenberg is another designer synonymous with the era. Glamorous black-and-white photos show her at the club, cigarette in hand and a flower in her hair. Born in Brussels, she became an apprentice to Angelo Ferretti, an Italian textile manufacturer, in 1969. In 1972, she opened her own business in New York. Her signature wrap dress, designed in 1973, became a best-seller. Made from jersey,

The jewellery designer's first success came when Roy Halston, who became her close friend, featured her work in his collections. Born in Florence, Peretti worked as a model in New York before turning to jewellery design. She was part of the in-crowd at Studio 54, the club that was fast becoming known for its cocaine-fuelled scenes.

it had long sleeves and a skirt to wrap around the body and tie. Apparently, the dress was inspired by a wrap top and skirt Julie Nixon Eisenhower had worn on TV in the early 1970s, and DVF combined the two pieces into one garment. It was a go-anywhere dress, sexy and arguably easy to move in.

Stephen Burrows

For American fashion designer Stephen Burrows, Studio 54 was all about sexy clothes – which he was certainly designing. Burrows, who studied at Philadelphia Museum College of Art and New York's Fashion Institute of Technology (FIT), went to work for the New York department store Henri Bendel – a 'Stephen Burrows World' boutique opened at the store in 1970 – but left in 1973 to open a design house. He is best known for his supple and comfortable leisurewear and body-conscious garments that were perfect for the disco scene. He was interested in the stretch of knit. A signature of his was visible stitching, which he used on hemlines of skirts to create a fluted shape, also known as a 'lettuce' edge or effect.

Stephen Sprouse

An apprentice to Halston, Sprouse was known best in the 1980s for his pop sensibility and vibrant clothes in bright fluro colours. Deemed inspirational as well as unconventional, graffiti was also a hallmark of the designer, whose brand would go in and out of business at the end of the 1980s. A collaboration with Louis Vuitton, then helmed by Marc Jacobs, put his name on the map again in the early noughties, before he passed away in 2004.

Norma Kamali

Though Kamali is highly associated with Studio 54, she has said she never actually went to the club (though rumour has it, she had been invited to do a fashion show there). The crowds that frequented the club wore her bodysuits and clothes to dance in, while its bouncers wore her, now famous, Sleeping Bag coats when on the door. Kamali, who has enjoyed much success over the decades and was responsible for innovating many of its best-known contemporary designs, has noted that Studio elevated fashion designers to celebrity status – something that, 50 years later, fashion has come to experience once again, through social media.

How it ended

The success and excess of Studio 54 came to an abrupt end. The owners were convicted of tax evasion and so ended the hedonism. But DVF's wrap dress lived on, Peretti landed a job at Tiffany, and Halston ended up leaving his label. He had sold the name to Norton Simon Inc in 1973, and while he remained as the principal designer, he later signed a contract to design an affordable clothing line for the mass retailer J C Penney. The move significantly damaged his career at the time, even though such collaborations are commonplace and actively encouraged in fashion today.

The condensed idea
Glamour, hedonism and excess

34 Japanese Wave

The arrival of Japanese designers in Paris in the early 1970s, and again in the 1980s and 1990s, introduced the Western world to key names who would shape, and shake up, the future of fashion. They included Kenzo Takada, Issey Miyake, Yohji Yamamoto, Rei Kawakubo, and more recently, Junya Watanabe, Noir Kei Ninomiya and Tao Kurihara – three of Kawakubo's protégés.

To this day, Japanese designers are known for their innovation, craft techniques, prevalent use of black, and avant-garde approach to design which, pertinently, challenges Western traditions of tailoring. Sleeves are not necessarily sleeves, or jackets jackets, in their hands, and a collaged approach to the body is often explored. Focus has often been on a layering and wrapping of the figure in unstructured garments or, conversely, shrouding and expounding the body entirely in conceptual styles. Such concepts have gained cult following in the fashion and art worlds.

The first wave

Kenzo Takada was born in Japan in 1939 and, along with Issey Miyake, was part of the first wave of influential Japanese designers to make it big. He studied at Bunka Fashion College, Tokyo, in 1958 before moving to Paris around 1964–65 where, in 1970, he opened his first boutique, named Jungle Jap. The same year, he debuted a collection that featured brightly coloured dresses that caught the eye and praise of *Elle* magazine.

A collection in 1973–74 saw skirts layered one upon another and wrapped with belts that had a folkloric feel to them – folklore, or his version of it, often inspired Takada and can be seen in subsequent collections. Takada drew on shapes from the kimono, preferring to use bold lines over darts. He mixed bright prints and colours with quilting techniques and intarsia knits. The latter re-emerged as a speciality and cult emblem for the brand around 2011–19 when Carol Lim and Humberto Leon, founders of the influential Opening Ceremony store in New York, became creative directors of Kenzo. By that time, the luxury goods conglomerate LVMH had bought Kenzo and rebranded it for a youthful, streetwear kind of customer.

The kimono

A longstanding sartorial symbol of Japan, the kimono is a form of traditional dress that has been worn by men and women of all classes of society since the 16th century, according to London's Victoria and Albert Museum, which celebrated the garment's influence on fashion in an exhibition that ran in 2020.

The wrap style allows for ease of movement. Introduced to Europe in the late 19th and early 20th centuries, the garment became fashionable as an alternative to the tea gown and was also often worn as a dressing gown.

Issey Miyake is a name best known for the designer's use of pleats and architectural shapes in bright, playful colours, or just black, around the body. Forms were unexpected, often inspired by nature, incorporating folds and twists and combining Eastern and Western elements together. Conversely, Miyake was also known for his comfortable clothing.

Born in Hiroshima, Miyake made his first fashion collection in 1963, before studying in Paris at L'Ecole de la Chambre Syndicale de la Couture Parisienne. He worked as a design assistant to Guy Laroche and Hubert de Givenchy before going on to design ready-to-wear for Geoffrey Beene in New York. He established his own label in 1970, and, from 1973, started to present in Paris twice yearly. Pleats became an integral part of his work, and in 1993 he introduced the Pleats Please Issey Miyake range, still incredibly popular, and known for its easy-breezy, wearable designs.

The second wave

Alongside Issey Miyake, who was still showing in Paris at the time, Yohji Yamamoto and Rei Kawakubo of Comme des Garcons made up the second Japanese wave of the 1980s. Some of their garments were inspired by traditional Japanese workwear or ceremonial clothes, others were more avant-garde. Their style is typically associated with a loose fit and omitting the body's natural shape.

Steve Jobs

Among Issey Miyake's most famous fans was Apple co-founder Steve Jobs, known for wearing mock turtleneck sweaters. According to the designer's obituary in *The New York Times*, Jobs and Miyake became good friends. The garment, it is inferred, appealed to the businessman and inventor because of its simplicity. Jobs made the garment by Miyake so famous that other tech-industry founders were soon seen wearing it, most notably Theranos founder Elizabeth Holmes.

While Miyake is known for geometric shapes, drape and flow, Yamamoto favoured unstructured and loose tailoring, often with additional pockets and straps. Kawakubo's designs were oversized, non-traditional, torn and crumpled pieces, which sometimes prompted confusion.

Born in Tokyo, Kawakubo studied fine arts and literature at Keio University. She went on to work at the Japanese textile company Asahi Kasei before becoming a freelance fashion designer. She founded Comme des Garcons, originally a line for women, in 1969. The men's line followed later in 1978, and the first Comme des Garcons show took place in Paris in 1981. Initially her collections, which challenged the social construct of women by experimenting with deconstruction techniques and distressed materials, reportedly caused outcry and the designer has said her critics got her work all wrong when they referred to it as 'ragged chic' or 'Hiroshima chic'. A Comme des Garcons fashion show is not like any other. There is a sense of calm and quiet and keen interest from the press and buyers to know what is going through Kawakubo's mind – as though she has answers to the big questions in life.

Kawakubo is thought of as a retail genius; the brand has various diffusion lines, which are far more accessible and wearable than the catwalk counterparts, and in 2008, Comme did a collaboration with the high-street brand H&M, some time before collaborations between luxury fashion and high-street names became commonplace.

Deconstructionism

Japanese designers, much like the Belgians who came after them, are associated with deconstruction fashion, which gained popularity during the 1980s. The aim was to draw attention to a garment's construction and to show off the parts of it that are typically being hidden and only come to light when a garment is damaged, has decomposed or disintegrated or been distressed. Visible seams, linings and raw edges are part of the aesthetic and there may be a collage element if the garment has been taken apart and put back together.

Street style

Off the catwalk, Japan is known for its highly influential street style, courtesy of the 1997 magazine *FRUiTS*, founded by Shoichi Aoki, which came along before the online street-style imagery of social media. Showcasing the coolest and most interesting looks of the time, in 2001 Phaidon published a book version of *FRUiTS*, which became a fashion bible as well as an insight into another world of fashion.

The condensed idea
Challenging Western ways
of dressing

35 New Romantics

The 1980s was a decade full of extremes and exaggerations in fashion, especially in London – from Goth to rave and power dressing, to the more wild and whimsical 'New Romantic' movement. The last is a term that was supposedly coined by the media, others have said music management, for young people towards the end of the 1970s and 1980s who dressed in reaction to the punk movement. It also came in the face of city-slick suits.

It was an elaborate and extravagant dressing-up-box style for clothes that bordered on costumes borrowed straight from history, fantasy and the future, fusing them altogether. Genderless ideas were readily accepted as were dyed hair and cosmetics for men and women. The look was an antidote to the confrontational street style that had come before, and was more sensationalist, if anything, than aggressive in aesthetic. It marked a move on from the 1970s, the beginning of a new era. The Now Crowd, Blitz Kids, Romantic Rebels and New Dandies are also names associated with this eclectic breed of style mavens.

Theatrical design

Fashion designers Vivienne Westwood and John Galliano are linked with the style – Westwood for her swashbuckling Pirate collection in 1981, which featured ensembles inspired by the 18th century – tricorn hats, oversized shirts with billowing sleeves, sashes and baggy-crotch trousers; and Galliano for his 1984 Les Incroyables collection, inspired by garments from the French Revolution. Galliano's collection was snapped up by Browns, a legendary boutique on London's South Molton Street, which was responsible for launching the careers of many young fashion designers over the years, including Alexander McQueen.

The New Romantic mood was encapsulated by historical and theatrical-looking pieces, a nostalgia and romance for the past, but was also tied up heavily with music and London's club scene, which was emerging as a new and edgy subculture – though it is the music, it has been observed, that took the whole thing mainstream.

Spandau Ballet, Duran Duran, Culture Club and Adam and the Ants were all key names on the music scene. Boy George, who was a founding member of Culture Club in 1981, with his dandy-androgyny, beautiful make-up, coloured long hair and layered clothes, epitomized this creative, soft and feminine style, which today is instantly recognizable as being from this era.

London

The UK capital was an important hub of the New Romantic scene. It was where the bands were forming, where the cool art kids were studying and where new clubs were emerging to show all of this off. Radical ideas and new talent were coming from Central Saint Martins and the Royal College of Art. They were coming from the Blitz nightclub, too. Started by

> We were young, full of our own self-importance, getting far more attention than we deserved, and far less than we wanted.
> Boy George

Steve Strange and Rusty Egan in 1979, the Blitz Club, located in Covent Garden, was famous for a door policy that was all about 'the weird and wonderful'. There is a story that Mick Jagger was refused entry because he was wearing jeans, a baseball cap and trainers. Access denied!

Anyone who was anyone went to the Blitz Club and you would find bands hanging out there alongside art students – David Bowie reportedly turned up looking to pluck a few from the crowd for his 'Ashes to Ashes' video in which he was dressed as Pierrot the clown –

Creativity capital

It is poignant that the British Fashion Council was established in 1983, staging its first London Fashion Week the following year. Out of the four fashion weeks (New York, London, Milan and Paris), it is London that is known for its new ideas, its young designers and a verve for creative output. The boom of creativity during the 1980s surely laid the foundations for this reputation, and at the time international designers would come to the city in search of inspiration. Still, to this day, international luxury fashion houses hire talent from London to lead their labels.

A fashion-movement ushered in by swooshes of hair and make-up (either experimental or conceptual), the New Romantic music scene was characterized by synthesizers and tracks such as 'Do You Really Want to Hurt Me' (Culture Club), 'To Cut a Long Story Short' (Spandau Ballet), 'Kings of the Wild Frontier' (Adam and the Ants, 'Planet Earth' (Duran Duran), 'Fade to Grey' (Visage), 'Calling Your Name' (Marilyn) and 'Poison Arrow' (ABC).

as well as future important media types such as *i-D* magazine's Dylan Jones, *Elle*'s Iain R Webb, master milliner Stephen Jones and fashion designer Pam Hogg. Stephen Jones, who has since become responsible for designing headwear for all of the best fashion houses from Dior to Marc Jacobs, told *The Guardian* in 2009 that he saw people at the Blitz Club he thought were only possible in his imagination. Clubs Billy's and Hell were also part of the scene, though Blitz is the best known.

The 1980s was the decade in which style titles – grass-roots and rebellious versions of the fashion glossies – such as *i-D* and *The Face* were launched. They were known especially for their avant-garde art direction and championing new talent. There was a raw energy to them, which mirrored what was happening in London among this new generation of creatives. In 1983, a textile design group called The Cloth formed at the Royal College of Art, design group with the aim of creating a dialogue between art and design projects, which included designing record sleeves for bands. Pam Hogg, known for provocative designs often worn by singers, opened her first concession at Hyper Hyper fashion on London's Kensington High Street in 1984.

> No longer a weekly secret society, the Blitz became a publicity machine for the pose age. Attendance became a statement of intent – to lead a life of style seven days a week.
>
> David Johnson, *The Guardian*

While the fashions would eventually fade, the New Romantics had a lasting impact on the way London's emerging designers fuse fashion with nightlife to create communities around their brands. Some 25 years later, another London-born nightlife fashion scene centred around clubs such as BoomBox, which instituted a similar dress code. It chimed with the birth of Nu Rave, or New Rave, a music scene linked to Klaxons, which was soon co-opted by London's East End, which defined fashion from around 2005–07 in bright colours and hedonistic outfits. Designers Henry Holland, Gareth Pugh and Cassette Playa were linked to this new iteration, while, more recently, Charles Jeffrey and Matty Bovan have promoted similar avant-garde community-based styles.

The condensed idea
London as the creative hub

36 The Belgians

When the renowned fashion journalist Suzy Menkes recalls the Belgian fashion designers of the 1980s, she has said, she thinks of recycling, oversize cutting, raw seams and a cerebral – or intelligent and serious – attitude. At the time they represented a significant contrast to the prevailing and excessive styles of the decade, a time of power dressing, the New Romantics and many different styles at once.

First arriving on the scene in the 1980s, Belgian designers have played a pivotal role in fashion ever since. They are known for their innovation, craftsmanship and cult designs, earning several of them top spots at some of fashion's most prestigious houses (Menkes also notes part of their power was being able to permeate the Paris houses), while others have chosen to stay independent and niche. It all began with the Antwerp Six.

The Antwerp Six

Dries Van Noten, Ann Demeulemeester, Walter Van Beirendonck, Dirk Bikkembergs, Dirk Van Saene and Marina Yee were the designers who made up the famous Antwerp Six. In 1986, they took their designs to a London fashion fair where, according to various recollections, it did not go so well to begin with as they had been put on a floor with bridalwear – quite a contrast to their own designs. Unhappy about this, the designers made some flyers to hand out at the entrance, and this led to a buyer from New York department store Barneys taking interest in their work and introducing them to the American market. The story goes that the press had such trouble pronouncing their Flemish names, that one of the group said, 'Just call us the Antwerp Six'.

> Antwerp is a city with a small-town feel, where everyone seems to know each other, but it punches way above its weight when it comes to culture.
>
> Eugene Rabkin, highsnobiety.com

Style-wise, the designers had little in common with each other. Instead, it was a similar youthful attitude, energy and approach to rethinking fashion that united them, it is noted. Among the best known on the international stage are Dries Van Noten and Ann Demeulemeester, whose collections are regularly

Antwerp Royal Academy of Fine Arts

The Antwerp Six designers all graduated from the city's Royal Academy of Fine Arts, an incubator of international talent. In the early 1980s, the final year of some of the designers' studies, there debuted a new award, called the Golden Spindle, to promote Belgian fashion. Demeulemeester won the competition in 1982, with her fellow Antwerp colleagues winning it at various points afterwards.

More recent graduates from the school include Balenciaga's creative director Demna Gvasalia, and Diesel/Y-Project's Glenn Martens. All of which has meant that, each graduating year, all eyes from press, buyers and talent scouts look to the school for the new wave of Belgian, or Belgian-trained, talent.

shown at Paris Fashion Week. Today, Dries is recognized for his vivid colour palette and ability to make infinitely wearable but emotional clothes, while Demeulemeester is known for a moodier take on fashion. In March 2024, it was announced that Dries Van Noten would be stepping down from his label – he had already sold a majority stake to the luxury group Puig in 2018 – much to the upset of the fashion industry.

A second wave

Lieve Van Gorp, Patrick van Ommeslaeghe, Jurgi Persoons, Angelo Figus, Veronique Branquinho and An Vandevorst and Filip Arickx of A F Vandevorst are among the names attributed to the second wave of Belgians, having graduated in the late 1980s to late 1990s. A F Vandevorst and Veronique Branquinho, whose designs centre on distressed and deconstructed looks and historical style, are among the better known.

Martin Margiela

One Belgian designer, much revered and widely celebrated, is not part of the Antwerp Six, although he is often mentioned in association with them: Martin Margiela. After graduating from the

Royal Academy of Fine Arts in 1980, Margiela headed to Paris to fulfil a childhood ambition to be a designer there. He landed a job as an assistant designer at Jean Paul Gaultier in 1984, and developed his own designs on the side. In 1987, he left Gaultier to make his own brand with business partner Jenny Meirens, showing their first collection later that year, for spring/summer 1989, in Paris. The

An ongoing legacy

Since The Antwerp Six, there have been other notable Belgian names in the world of fashion. The ever-influential Raf Simons worked in furniture before launching a menswear label in 1995 – which he did self-trained, inspired by youth culture and traditional menswear. In 2005, he was appointed creative director at Jil Sander (menswear and womenswear), where he was noted for his sensual minimalism. The show, which took place during Milan Fashion Week, was one of the hottest tickets of the season. Among his most memorable womenswear collections was for spring/summer 2011: white T-shirts were worn with ball-gown-style skirts in a very low-key way that could be widely adopted for everyday wear. He left in 2012, next heading to Christian Dior, then Calvin Klein and subsequently Prada. Simons is a designer's designer, and many look to him to see what will happen next.

Kris Van Assche, also a menswear designer, spent time at Dior Homme from 2007–18, where he brought rebellious spirit to the brand. In his wake, Matthieu Blazy and Pieter Mulier (formerly Raf Simons' right-hand man) have become contemporary Belgian names to know. The former for his work with Italian brand Bottega Veneta and the latter with legendary Alaïa. Both houses are known for their craftsmanship and have enjoyed renewed interest and success following these appointments.

Olivier Theyskens, meanwhile, has carved out a successful career with his own label, known for its historic, dark and romantic references, as well as at Paris houses including Nina Ricci and Rochas, and the US-based brand Theory.

event has become the stuff of legend with everyone in fashion claiming to have been there.

Margiela is known for his deconstructed and DIY spirit of garments, in which seams on show are championed rather than shamed. There is a dishevelled beauty to the garments. In recent years, it was Margiela who introduced the world to the tabi shoe, which resembles an animal hoof and has become a cult-now-popular footwear design. It is also Margiela whose name is most associated with being a deconstructionist, an idea that both the Belgians and Japanese embraced.

The condensed idea
The birth of moody, angst-focused fashion

37 Power Dressing

Dressing for success was about getting ahead and, for women, that meant being taken seriously in the workplace, signalled through their clothes. Power dressing, as it became known, emerged in the late 1970s but was most prevalent during the 1980s. It was about dressing with confidence and with an authoritative look that relied upon wearing tailored suiting to take on the boardroom, which was typically full of men at that time. Such was the wardrobe of the emerging career woman, a new species of female who placed more importance on her job than she did being stuck in the kitchen cooking, and who was starting to find a valid place in many facets of life.

In 1979, Margaret Thatcher became the first female prime minister in the United Kingdom, a landmark moment for the visibility of women in positions of power, regardless of political allegiance. The Iron Lady, as she was called, was known for reliably dressing in a skirt suit with a pussy bow blouse and carrying a proper handbag; she was an expert at power dressing. So, too, were the female characters of the 1981 American soap opera *Dynasty*. Its protagonists – including Alexis Carrington Colby, played by Joan Collins – promoted the trend for wide shoulders. *Miami Vice* did the same for menswear in 1984, while Melanie Griffith as Tess McGill in the 1988 film *Working Girl* became a poster girl for the career woman. McGill works in a cutthroat office environment in New York and the film's strong female characters wore strong shoulder pads to match.

> Dressing poorly does not destroy a man's career the way it does a woman's.
>
> *New Women's Dress for Success,* John T Molloy

In fashion publishing, there was another fierce character of note: Anna Wintour, who took the helm of British *Vogue* in 1985. Her modus operandi was to target the new 1980s businesswoman, who was busy and time-poor, presumably much like Wintour herself. Her approach would take her next to the lead role at American *Vogue* in 1988.

The new 1980s female icon was financially independent as well as sexually liberated and had the means to buy a wardrobe that

The Woman's Dress for Success Book, John T Molloy

The image consultant John T Molloy debuted *The Woman's Dress for Success Book* in 1977–78, a book for women with, it claimed, backed-up recommendations on how women's clothes at work influenced what they earned. A men's version had been published in 1975. He pointed out that the right clothing had power and could give a woman the edge. He was talking about power dressing. Other books by Molloy on the subject include: *Dress for Success* (1975), *Live for Success* (1981) and *New Women's Dress for Success* (1996).

reflected all of this. Designers and fashion houses happily obliged. (The 1980s is also noted as being a significant time for the emergence of big brands and logos.)

The look? Big shoulders via shoulder pads, peplums, jackets with matching mini-skirts, stiletto heels, big hair. The mini-skirts of the1980s were not the mini-skirts of the 1960s, however. Worn with heels they commanded the room, rather than blending into it. Accessories mattered: big earrings and big bangles, a belt to cinch the waist, a chain-strap handbag (think Chanel).

Some 40 years later, combined, these components are immediately identifiable as belonging to the era of 1980s power dressing – to the point that referencing them now becomes almost pastiche. It is an idea that Demna Gvasalia, of the fashion house Balenciaga, has explored. Caricature-like shoulders have featured in many collections and have become something of a signature for the brand under his watch, taken to borderline absurd proportions. The trope of office wear has been turned on its head as an ironic high-fashion offering.

Leading the way

Claude Montana and Thierry Mugler were among the key proponents of the original inverted triangle silhouette (though it should be noted that a triangle shape was part of the 1930s silhouette, as well as the 1940s – think of the femmes fatales of film noir, who wore ensembles of jackets with padded shoulders and nipped-in waists and body-

The 1980s was the decade of the yuppy. Short for 'young urban professional' or 'young upwardly mobile professional', the yuppy was born between 1946 and 1964 and worked in the cities at high-paying jobs. They aspired to a certain kind of lifestyle and wore classic clothes and had iconic accessories, such as the Rolex watch, the Filofax organizer and Gucci loafers. Yuppies were defined by their jobs as well as their clothes.

hugging skirts). Mugler was regarded as a stylist as much as a designer. His garments were confident, bold and strong in shape, taking their influence from the 1940s and also the fashions of the 1950s. Shoulders were exaggerated, as were waists and hips.

The Italian, Giorgio Armani, made a name for himself with his tailoring, which was a more subtle take on power dressing, with softer padded shoulder lines, but that nevertheless conveyed sophistication and professionalism; and American designer Donna Karan invented the 'seven easy pieces'.

Karan's was equally a less aggressive form of workwear and targeted the urban professional woman who was time-poor. Constructed from stretch fabrics, the pieces were body-conscious and included a wrapped skirt, an all-in-one body and tubular dress styles. While he was working at Chanel, appointed there in 1983, the late Karl Lagerfeld constantly reinvented the famous Chanel suit, which in its day had been a revolutionary design – possibly the first power suit.

> The suit has been raised by men to a special position
>
> *New Women's Dress for Success,* John T Molloy

Off the catwalk, everyone from the late Diana, Princess of Wales, to Michael Jackson was embracing the boxy silhouette of power dressing. The look is datable but what makes it important is the psychology behind it. Men had long been wearing suits at work but women had not. Power dressing changed this and made them more equal. And it empowered women to enter the boardroom, feel as though they belonged and could, in business speak, break the glass ceiling. Today, power dressing is considered anything that makes the wearer feel confident and does not necessarily relate to tailoring, or big shoulders.

Girlboss

Since the mid-2010s, the term 'girlboss' has been used to describe an ambitious and successful woman, particularly an entrepreneur. The term was defined more by an attitude than it is a style of dressing. In recent years, though, the term has started to take on negative associations.

The condensed idea
Look powerful, be powerful

38 Minimalism vs Maximalism

Fashion designers and houses typically fall into one of two categories: minimalist – refined and considered lines, perceivably practical; or maximalist – bold, a spectacle, perceivably impractical. And they tend not to deviate from that style, no matter what trends are or are not happening.

Less is more

The term 'minimalism' is noted as first being used in a fashion context in the mid-1980s, to describe a trend for lean, pared-down clothing in neutral tones (beige, navy), inspired by the clean, sculptural shapes of the Japanese designers showing their collections in Europe. It refers to garments that are rigorous in their design and fabrications often incorporate intellectual concepts of dressing and utility.

Contemporary designers that fall into this category are The Row, founded by the Olsen twin sisters and poster girls for the quiet luxury trend, Phoebe Philo, formerly of Celine (at the time Céline) fame, Raf Simons and Prada where Simons became co-artistic director in 2020.

The trend began, however, with Calvin Klein, who is often the first name that springs to mind when talking about minimalism. Interestingly, it does seem to be mostly US designers who are minimalists – it chimes with their roots in sportswear, ready-to-wear and collegiate styles.

The Americans

Born in New York, Calvin Klein graduated from the Fashion Institute of Technology (FIT) in 1962 and from 1964–68 worked for various coat and suit manufacturers before starting his own business. He specialized in designing coats and suits, but during the mid-1970s, gained a reputation for his soft tailoring and clean lines. He would further become known for long, slimline and non-fussy jackets, blazers and blouses. His preferred textiles included silk, linen and wools – essentially luxurious fabrics that brought with them a minimalist attitude. His designs did not feature overt decoration or lean into whimsy. He is noted for saying that he wanted to make simple and comfortable but stylish clothes.

In the 1990s, the designer cemented this minimalist aesthetic, popularizing the slip dress. He also proffered the idea of designer jeans (first introduced during the 1970s, and back in fashion again during the 1990s) and then underwear, which, hugely successful, promoted an androgynous and unisex style.

Before Klein was Bill Blass, who had studied at Parsons in New York in 1939. After World War II, he worked for the fashion house Anna Miller & Co, later buying the company in 1970 and renaming it Bill Blass. It would become known for traditional garments with softened lines and a nonchalant American attitude.

Giorgio and Jil

Italian designer Giorgio Armani, along with Calvin Klein and German designer Jil Sander, are considered purists as opposed to minimalists, some say. They use beige and grey tones, architectural and geometric forms and are known for their restrained, or understated, sense of style. Pieces are pragmatic and unpretentious; they are functional because they have been reduced only to what is needed.

Cause and effect

When a recession hits, commentators in fashion expect designers to react in one of two ways: with a move towards minimalism, to mirror the eco-socio landscape at large, or towards maximalism, because why not if everything is so bad?

As a rule of thumb, in everything from science to art, such moves are linked to what came before. And trends typically tend to occur in reaction against one another. After the millennium, when fashion went silver and white, utilitarian and slick, there came boho, which was frilly and pretty and layered and handmade. The space-age styles of the 1960s, were followed by 1970s folk and hippy fashion. The logic follows, therefore, that a minimalist era will be followed by a maximalist one – which can mean anything from colour palette to print and from surface decoration to shape and size – and vice versa.

Armani, best known for fluid tailoring and an affection for beige, was born in Piacenza, Italy. He studied medicine at Milan University and, after military service, joined the Italian department store chain La Rinascente as a window dresser. He next worked as a menswear designer at Nino Cerruti, turning freelance and establishing his own menswear collection in 1975. During the 1980s, he became one of the most influential designers owing to his menswear design sensibility, which he managed to adapt to womenswear. His designs were relaxed, elegant and contemporary in feel, resulting in a timeless quality. The designer is also known for classics.

Jiline Sander, known as the brand Jil Sander, was born in Wesselburen, Germany, where she studied textile design before heading off to Los Angeles as an exchange student. She first became a journalist before she became a designer, and opened a boutique in the late 1960s, in Hamburg, where she showed her first collection a few years later in the early 1970s. It was her minimalist style that garnered interest on the international scene – combining male garments, known for their simplicity, with luxurious fabrics to give a sense of the feminine. Emphasis was on the structure and shape of garments as opposed to decoration. Sander was one of the most influential fashion designers of the 1990s. The Belgian designer Raf Simons was creative director of the brand from 2005–12. His own style was ideally suited to the brand, a mix of masculine and considered design, which saw him become a much-loved figure in fashion and his collections at Jil Sander were always highly anticipated.

More is more

On the flip side of the minimalist is the maximalist designer or fashion house. Maximalism is the reaction to minimalism. It is about extravagance, drama, colour, the ornate and largely the impractical. Interestingly, while couture is often looked upon as being a fashion spectacle and some of its designs unwearable (each season, the question gets asked: Is there still a place for it), most of what actually gets made for clients is a toned-down version, often in black. Christian Lacroix, John Galliano, Jean Paul Gaultier and Vivienne Westwood can all be described as maximalist designers.

French Lacroix studied art history at Montpellier University and museum studies at the Sorbonne, Paris. He worked at Hermès, and

Patou as head of couture in 1981, opening his own house in Paris in 1987. His clothes confidently combined historic shapes with bright clashing colours, embroideries and prints. They were dramatic and thrilling. He no longer produces collections, and the fashion world has surely lost a true maker of fantasy and magic as a result.

John Galliano, one of fashion's original 'enfant terribles' (who worked at Givenchy, Dior and then Margiela), was also known for fantastical themes that took us swashbuckling through history, through literature and the geography of the world. The Central Saint Martins graduate was famous for his 1984 collection, Les Incroyables, which was inspired by the 18th-century clothing of France. His designs were romantic, whimsical and layered with imaginative references, taking clothes to costume levels.

Gaultier, too, has an enfant terrible reputation – the French designer created cone bras and corsets, showy designs full of humour and glamour, mixing old and new references – as, of course, did Vivienne Westwood. There was getting dressed and then there was dressing up, all of which these designers proffered.

While many of these minimalist and maximalist designers have run labels at the same time as one another, broadly speaking, the maximalists are predominantly associated with the 1980s and the minimalists with the 1990s.

The condensed idea
Reactionary fashion

39 Grunge

The term 'grunge' was first used by the fashion trade title *Women's Wear Daily* in 1992. It reflected a new mood in fashion that centred on anti-glamour. Ushered in by the American designer Marc Jacobs, it was rooted in music, magazines, youth culture and street style.

The antithesis of the supermodel era, grunge took inspiration from the new, raw music styles coming out of Seattle, with bands such as Nirvana, fronted by grunge pin-up Kurt Cobain, and Pearl Jam. Models Kate Moss, Karen Elson, Stella Tennant and Kristen McMenamy, were noted for a new and appealing quirkiness.

Style publications such as *i-D*, *The Face* and *Dazed & Confused* provided an alternative to mainstream reads and were as anti-glossy as grunge was anti-glamazon. These magazines set out to capture culture and subculture on the ground, and played around with subverting the format of the traditional fashion magazine. Graphics and art direction were experimental, with photographs of real people featuring alongside provocative fashion shots showcasing an indie way of life. It was exciting and aspirational in an entirely different way than had been seen before – and it was not always healthy.

When grunge emerged in the early 1990s it coincided with the controversial 'waif' look and 'heroin chic', which promoted worrying

---

The grunge look

Characterized by an overall dishevelled feel, the grunge look was made up of thrift shop, or vintage, finds and had evolved from street culture, teenagers and rock bands. It was anti-consumerist and political. Clothes such as cardigans and T-shirts were often oversized, cargo pants and jeans were torn and ripped or faded and likely too big, nightdresses were worn with beanies. It was a mix and mismatch with the flannel plaid shirt taking a starring role – arguably the item most associated with the trend, worn open over T-shirts. All of this would get a high-fashion makeover.

---

thinness, gauntness, a sense of self-destruction and a glamorization of drugs. Condemned by US President Bill Clinton in 1997, by the end of the decade a shift had taken place and magazines had moved away from creating such images.

Marc Jacobs

Jacobs is one of America's best-known fashion exports today. Not only has he had huge success in running his own labels, Marc Jacobs and Marc by Marc Jacobs, he was the first-ever ready-to-wear artistic director for the Paris fashion house Louis Vuitton, appointed in 1997. To many, he is best-known for introducing grunge to our wardrobes, and this began at Perry Ellis.

In 1989, Jacobs joined Perry Ellis as vice president of women's design. Perry Ellis was founded by Ellis himself, who designed under his own name from 1976, and was known as an American sportswear brand that did contemporary classic menswear. In his final year at Parsons School of Design in New York, in 1984, Jacobs created a collection of hand-knitted sweaters that won him the Perry Ellis Golden Thimble award. Working on his own label for a couple of years after graduation, he subsequently joined Perry Ellis in the late 1980s.

It was his spring/summer 1993 collection for the label that hit the headlines. A combination of youth culture and rock 'n' roll, in what would have been the street style of teenagers living in the Pacific Northwest, grunge was born – the opposite of Perry Ellis' preppy style. It was a groundbreaking collection in that respect, but a commercial failure (customers, it seems, weren't prepared to pay for this blend of dishevelled chic, even though Jacobs

> It was the collection that got Marc Jacobs fired from Perry Ellis. It was the show that made his career.
> vogue.com

had added finesse in the craftsmanship), which in some ways has only worked to cement its influential status in fashion history. The combinations of combat boots and little dresses and shirts made a huge impact and to this day, to see it is to see grunge.

Anna Sui is another designer whose aesthetic is noted as leaning into the grunge aesthetic, though typically more bohemian and colourful, feminine and vintage. Michigan-born, she also studied at Parsons and debuted her first runway show in 1991, inspired by hippie chic.

Just like punk that came before it, there was a shock-factor involved with grunge and, later, serious health concerns. Clothes looked pre-worn, dishevelled and had a 'just got out of bed' feel to them, which was a perplexing proposition for some consumers. It was also difficult for women over a certain age to wear, and with its layers and trailing fabrics was impractical.

On the flip side, the style has been praised for its liberating qualities – and certainly, looking back, it introduced an overall casualness to fashion that has never really left. A more updated version of grunge became a normcore trend in the mid-2010s, when the fashion brand Vetements shook up the fashion industry with its layered looks that put hoodies and flannel shirts back on fashion's agenda.

Kate Moss

Described as waif-like, Moss became a key face of grunge, particularly because of photographs taken of her by Corinne Day for *The Face* and British *Vogue*, which epitomized the anti-glamour mood, its simplicity and rawness. She appeared on the cover of *The Face* in 1990 in a shoot called 'The 3rd Summer of Love', in which she wore a feather headdress and can be seen giggling. The image was styled by Melanie Ward, who has described that era as being one of great change, and a time of freedom to express yourself. It is among several well-known images of Moss that are synonymous with grunge. Another is her 1993 shoot with Day for British *Vogue*. The young Moss was photographed leaning against a white wall with fairy lights nonchalantly following her silhouette against it. Stark, powerful – and prompting accusations that Day was promoting heroin chic and anorexia.

> Even the kids in Seattle threatened to wash their hair in protest of having their look co-opted by a gang of gorgeous supermodels.
> Cathy Horyn, *The Cut*

Day was not the only photographer known for this bleak, or stark, documentary style of shooting. Juergen Teller, David Sims and Terry

Richardson also fit into this category, which was popular during the grunge era. In common with the fashion, it was about making the mundane interesting.

Grunge evolution

Indie sleaze is perhaps the most recent iteration of grunge. Its own mini-fashion era, it is pegged to the late 2000s and early 2010s, as a sexy-messy update on grunge, centred on skinny jeans, leather jackets, little dresses worn with tights, messed-up hair and messed-up make-up, as though you were perhaps still out from the night before. Pin-ups of the style include Pete Doherty and Kate Moss, always at Glastonbury, as well as Alexa Chung. It was a look indulged by Hedi Slimane at Saint Laurent to great effect.

The condensed idea
Paving the way for a more casual way of dressing

40 Androgyny and Gender

In fashion, androgyny has typically referred to possessing both male and female characteristics, or possessing neither. Examples cited include women with short bob-style haircuts, wearing tailored suits, for example, or men adopting more traditionally 'feminine' styles, considered as wearing hair long, make-up, jewellery, and clothes with more colour or ornate decoration.

Yet, as pointed out by fashion academic Elizabeth Wilson, until the 17th or 18th centuries, sexual difference in dress was not strongly marked and both men and women continued to dress alike. Gender difference, she notes, was more clearly established during the industrial period.

The late James Laver, a leading authority in the United Kingdom on fashion and costume, noted that women were less ornately dressed than men around the Middle Ages and that fashion/costume history has largely tracked clothing through the lens of menswear and womenswear, which have been demarcated by trousers for men and skirts for women.

Masculine versus feminine

Reviewers, critics, stylists, designers and even shoppers find themselves describing clothes as being more masculine or more feminine, meaning they pertain to have qualities or an appearance that is traditionally associated with the respective gender. For example, power dressing was a more masculine way for women to dress, while the New Romantic mode was a more feminine way for men to dress. Fashion as a means has been a way to define gender and negotiate its bounds. The French term *la garçonne* translates as 'boyish' and means someone who dresses in the opposite way to how women are expected to dress. The expression 'gamine' similarly refers to a woman who is boyish and elegant. A 'dandy' refers to a man who is overly concerned with his fashionable appearance. In recent years, designers have increasingly explored non-binary fashion designs and ideas.

Gender has played an interesting role in the evolution of fashion: defining it, building it, rejecting it, subverting it. The latter could be a definition of androgyny. In talking about androgyny in fashion, various names come up as ambassadors of its 'style' early on. They include Marlene Dietrich, Greta Garbo, Katharine Hepburn and, later, the fictional character Annie Hall, played by Diane Keaton.

Garbo and Dietrich were actresses among the Golden Age of Hollywood. Swedish-born Garbo was known for her shoulder-length hair and penchant for slouch hats and trench coats, clean lines and impeccably tailored coats. German Dietrich appropriated male attire more directly and was spotted in 1933 wearing a masculine suit in Paris. She wore hats, neckties, brogues and trousers, and accessorized an outfit with a cigar. She was known to wear her trousers both on and off screen for publicity shoots, as well as in her private life. Apparently, during her 1933 Paris visit, she had been warned by the police that she was liable for prosecution for her attire, referring to an order from 1800 when female-to-male cross-dressing was forbidden.

During the late 1970s, Keaton's Annie Hall wore waistcoats and slacks, ties and blazers and looked almost as though an incarnation of Chanel's masculine looks. These outfits were the antithesis of the female stereotype at the time.

Yves Saint Laurent

It was under Yves Saint Laurent's watchful eye that the tuxedo became mainstream for women as a fashion item, widely referred to as Le Smoking. In his hands, the traditionally male suit featured in a landmark moment when shown on his haute-couture runway in 1966, though the designer had not entirely copied a man's tuxedo, instead taking the same codes and adapting them for a woman. Alongside the little black dress, it is considered one of the most important inventions – or adaptations – in fashion history, arguably a precursor to power dressing. The designer himself is famous for noting the success of Le Smoking as being to do with style, not fashion, which he said easily came and went, while style stays.

Saint Laurent further presented the safari trouser suit in 1968, which pushed the boundaries of what was considered appropriate

The necktie

While the accessory initially started out as being a key component of men's formalwear – evolving to its more familiar form in the late 19th century – at the end of the 19th century, as a trend, women also began wearing neckties with blouses. They would again be popular with women among the unisex styles of the 1960s and 1970s. And ties became part of the pop-punk alternative rock scene, as worn by the singer Avril Lavigne.

for women to wear during the day, and he would continue to show variations of Le Smoking throughout his career – and many other designers would also be inspired by it.

Glam rock

Marc Bolan, of the British band T-Rex, proffered flamboyant suits, long hair, sequin and glitter during the early 1970s; David Bowie introduced us to his androgynous alter-ego Ziggy Stardust in 1972, dressed in skin-tight catsuits, one-legged leotards, and bright red hair. Glam rock was known for its theatrical and eccentric style, which blurred the gender boundary lines and cast men in clothes that were ornate and seemingly impractical. Both boys and girls flirted with platform boots of towering heights. Barbara Hulanicki's famous Biba store championed unisex glamour – feather boas hung from all the hat stands that paraded as the rails. All the stars of the day could be found shopping there.

It was from this world that Alessandro Michele, former creative director at Gucci, seemed to borrow. In 2015, in a sudden and surprising move, the Italian fashion house appointed its new leader from inside the house (as opposed to appointing a big name from outside, which is typically what happens).

Michele's debut show for Gucci, which he was rumoured to have made in five days following the exit of Frida Giannini, was full of delicate blouses, pussy bows, pretty printed suiting, lace and men who wore the same wistful looks. Whether it intended to or not, it borrowed from the 1970s; it was glam rock for the modern age, it was androgynous and it set fashion's agenda for the next seven years, until Michele left the brand in 2022. While there, he collaged his collections together in terms of colour and references.

It was maximalism at its best – maximalism, author and fashion and media consultant Marnie Fogg, points out, enables gender ambiguity. Indeed, when Michele came along, the term 'gender fluid' started to be used on a regular basis. As James Laver notes, clothes have typically been tailored to fit the body of a man or a woman, whereas the idea of gender fluid, non-binary and gender neutral is not as restrictive. Gucci was also among the first brands to introduce co-ed shows – co-ed being when the menswer and womenswear are shown together in one show, or collection, as opposed to separately.

The condensed idea
Blurring and breaking boundaries

41 The Sandal

Sandals are a summer staple. Each season, designs vary beyond the original definition, depending on what is in fashion – gladiator style, flatforms, flip-flops, kitten heels – but the sandal's history goes back far beyond the whims of the fashion calendar.

Defined as a type of footwear that consists of a sole secured to the foot using straps over the instep (the top part of the foot between the ball and ankle), ankle or toes, sandals appear to be the oldest known type of shoe. Since their first use, they have gained heels and platforms, buckles and zips, and straps added for decoration over function.

Best foot forward

There is climatic evidence to suggest that we were protecting our feet from harsh conditions by about 50,000 years ago and that we were using substantial soles around 40,000 years ago. The earliest existing examples of footwear are pairs of sandals, rather than shoes or boots, designed to protect the feet from extreme conditions encountered under foot – whether from heat or the cold.

Sagebrush bark sandals have been found in Oregon, dating back 10,900 years. In 2023, a pair made from esparto, a type of grass used for crafts, and dated to around 6,000 years old, was found in a bat cave in southern Spain. A total of 22 sandals were found in the cave. Some were described as having been worn, others not, with the suggestion that they were made for the dead. They did not feature laces but had a braid fixed to the middle that probably tied around the ankle. Similar styles of sandal found in Armenia are estimated to be 5,500 years old.

Socks and sandals

Among fashion's greatest debates is whether a person should wear socks with their sandals. Deemed by some to be a fashion faux pas, others see it as a quirky-chic trait. What was once the clichéd style choice of the stereotypical tourist has now become the preserve of the off-duty rich and famous.

Not everyone was allowed to wear early forms of footwear. In ancient Egypt, for example, only people of importance were allowed to wear them, or they were worn for special occasions. They were typically made of papyrus as well as materials such as leather and wood, but gold sandals have been found in Egyptian tombs. In its 2015 exhibition celebrating the history of shoes, the Victoria and Albert Museum showcased a sandal dating back to the late Pharaonic Egyptian, or early Roman, period. The earliest item of footwear in the whole exhibition, its insole was gilded with near-pure gold, but it apparently showed no signs of wear.

Wealthy ancient Greeks and Romans also wore sandals and indeed the Greek god Hermes is shown wearing winged sandals. Today, a popular sandal brand is called Ancient Greek and features wings as part of its signature design, the wings protruding from the ankle base. Greeks are thought to have worn footwear indoors only rarely and the poorer classes went barefoot. Only the wealthy wore sandals. Courtesans, it has been noted, sometimes wore sandals with studded soles that spelled out 'follow me' in the footprint.

> According to an ancient Greek myth, the gods and goddesses had their sandals made on the beautiful island of Crete by a gifted sandal maker who enriched each pair with magical powers.
>
> Ancient Greek Sandals

Fashion historian James Laver has pointed out that there is a very specific difference between ancient Greek and Etruscan attire, and that is the footwear. Until the 5th century BCE, when the influence of Greece led to them adopting sandals, the Etruscans had worn a high-laced boot with a turned-up toe.

A great many of the sandals popularized by fashion today have ancient origins. The gladiator style, for example, which features several wide straps holding the sole to the foot and one around the ankle, was introduced in the late 1960s (and has since seen modified iterations) was copied from those worn by Romans in the gladiator arena. Flip-flops, featuring a strap between the first and second toes, are based on the original Japanese sandal, the zori.

During the Middle Ages, it is thought that only peasants wore sandals, and in the 16th century, monks wore them in monastic orders. It was in the 1920s and 1930s, when women started to show off

Renowned Italian shoe designer Salvatore Ferragamo made show-stopping footwear. Among his most celebrated styles is the Rainbow sandal, created for Hollywood actress Judy Garland, in 1938. Boasting six stacks of colourful suede to form the cork wedge heel, it has gold straps, and has become an iconic design in footwear history. Ferragamo was known for creating shoes fit for stars, and this was exemplary of his magical style.

their feet more owing to the new, liberating flapper dress styles with short hems, that sandals were introduced as fashion items for eveningwear, sportswear and daywear. Following World War II, as with many things, societal rules had relaxed and it was more acceptable for women to show off their toes and heels.

Birkenstocks

Sandals have come a long way since their humble and mostly pragmatic beginnings. Among those that have stood the test of time is the Birkenstock. A family invention, the Birkenstock sandal that we know today (and which became increasingly popular in fashion in the late 2010s/early 2020s) came about when the great grandson of Johann Adam Birkenstock, Konrad, developed a 'footbed' – an evolved version of the insole that was designed to keep the foot healthy and comfortable.

Then, in 1954, Konrad's grandson Karl came up with the 'footbed sandal' design, which was released in 1963. Initially it was a failure, which is difficult to comprehend today, when the brand has since collaborated with high-fashion names that include Rick Owens, Jil Sander, Proenza Schouler and Manolo Blahnik.

Blahnik notably designed one of fashion's most powerful sandals – a slingback that the long-standing editor of American *Vogue*, Anna Wintour, wears regularly (so much so that Blahnik nicknamed the style the AW shoe, even though its official name is Callasli). Wintour is most often photographed wearing a nude pair, the theory being they go with everything.

Design classic

Jackie Kennedy made famous Capri's handmade sandals during a visit in the 1960s. She paid a visit to the island's Canfora shop – which makes made-to-measure sandals and counted Grace Kelly among its first customers – at midnight so that she could select her sandals in privacy.

Today, designers create some of the most magical footwear, especially sandals. For her spring/summer 2012 Prada show, Miuccia Prada sent high-heeled, flame-decorated sandals down the runway, playing into the collection's overall 1950s nostalgia, while the British footwear designer Sophia Webster specializes in creating colourful butterfly-like designs. Sandals have come quite some way since their very first outing.

The condensed idea
Protection and advancement

42 Jewellery

There seems to be no official date for when jewellery came to be used or made, though it has been worn for centuries, primarily as a form of decoration, but also as a type of talisman, a religious token, a sign of status or some sort of symbolic emblem – there are many reasons.

The ancient Egyptians wore collars made of beads and shells, and amulets of the scarab. Decorative items have been found in the tombs of both Cretan men and women. Pieces were used to pin and fasten clothes in place in ancient Greece and were worn increasingly during ancient Roman times, such as cameos, rings, anklets, earrings, headbands and bracelets. Earrings are mentioned in the Bible and are visible in historic carvings and on ancient monarchs. During the Bronze Age and the Iron Age, Celtic people of western Europe wore twisted metal collars, or torques (torcs).

Historically gold and silver are among the most popular metals used for making jewellery across the globe. More primitive materials have included included seeds, nuts, shells, teeth and claws strung on grass, while monarchs wore majestic gemstones, including diamonds, rubies, emeralds and sapphires.

Rings

Poison rings – literally devices for slipping poison into an enemy's goblet or plate – existed from ancient Roman times until the 17th century, later emerging as perfume rings. Signet rings were used to make an impression in sealing wax on letters. And wedding bands have been worn since ancient Egyptian times but were not adopted by Christians until the second half of the 9th century. The plain gold style we know today is said to come from Mary Tudor and her marriage to Philip II of Spain in 1554.

Through the ages

Medieval jewellery reflected status and hierarchy: royalty and nobility would wear gold, silver and precious gems, whereas those in lower ranks of society wore base metals such as copper and pewter. Before the late-14th century, gems were typically polished rather than cut and it was their size and colour that determined their value – factors that are still important today, known as the the 'four cs': cut, carat, colour and clarity. Goldsmiths were able to add colour to their jewellery using enamel.

During the Renaissance period (14th–17th centuries), jewellery was all about grandeur and impressiveness, and advances in cutting techniques meant that stones could be more sparkly. The mid-17th century saw the introduction of new styles of jewellery owing to changes in fashion, and gemstones were now more widely available thanks to an expanding global trade. Botanical and bow motifs are noted as being popular during this time.

Diamonds dominated 18th-century jewellery, serving as an essential component of court life. Interestingly, small swords

> Jewellery was man's answer to the profound human need for self-adornment and, consequently, is one of the oldest forms of decorative art.
>
> *7000 Years of Jewellery*, edited by Hugh Tait

were deemed an item of male jewellery because they were the product of a goldsmith and jeweller as opposed to a swordsmith. While the 19th century was a time of rapid industrial advancement, jewellery designs from this period often looked back to the past, referring to ancient Roman and Grecian styles and techniques. The look was overall naturalistic. It was also during the 19th century that Arts and Crafts designs emerged, rejecting the machine-led world and focusing on the handcrafting of individual pieces, which often had symbolic meaning.

The turn of the 20th century and then into the 1920s brought Art Nouveau and Art Deco styles of jewellery, respectively. The former was underpinned by organic, dark and erotic designs with languid lines, while the latter tended towards more geometric, modern designs. Jewellers and jewellery houses continued to explore techniques and materials well into the 1960s and have not stopped since. New ideas, fabrications and inventions have seen everything from textiles to paper

Cultural references

It was Marilyn Monroe who said that diamonds were a girl's best friend and immortalized the New York jewellery house Harry Winston (among others, including Tiffany & Co and Cartier), in the eponymous song from *Gentlemen Prefer Blondes* (1953). Audrey Hepburn, as Holly Golightly, brought the glittering word of Tiffany & Co to our attention in *Breakfast at Tiffany's* (1961) and the *Pink Panther* film franchise (1960s) fictionalized the underbelly of the diamond industry. Other films featuring impressive jewels include *High Society* (1956), *To Catch a Thief* (1955) and *Cleopatra* (1963).

used to make jewellery, and wander into wearable art territory, such as Paco Rabanne's chainmail dresses of the 1960s.

In recent years, lab-grown diamonds have become a popular business venture for a new wave of jewellers and some legacy houses have also started to dabble with the idea. Lab-grown diamonds do not come out of the earth but are created through a controlled process. Aesthetically, there is said to be very little difference, making them an attractive sustainable alternative. They can also be made quickly and are less expensive, on average, than natural diamonds.

Fine jewellery

London's Old Bond Street has long been filled with prestigious heritage jewellers whose designs use only precious metals and stones, among them Cartier, Chaumet, Harry Winston, Graff, David Morris, De Beers, Van Cleef & Arpels, Tasaki, Tiffany & Co, Boucheron, Garrard and Chanel. The windows glint with carats and cuts. It is at these houses that you will find famous stones, iconic designs and rare finds. The equivalent of Old Bond Street in Paris is Place Vendôme, which has a rich history of jewellers. It is the epicentre of jewellery and each house lays claim to having been the first to have arrived there. In the United States, it is New York's Fifth Avenue that has forever cemented itself as being home of the high-class jewellers, and is where Tiffany & Co can be found alongside the flagship stores of Cartier, Harry Winston and more.

Costume jewellery

The term 'costume jewellery' refers to pieces that are made from non-precious gemstones and metals, though they might well imitate them. Such pieces became popular in the West during the 1920s, largely owing to the French fashion house Chanel, although Schiaparelli is also associated with the trend. Chanel was well known for its imitation pearls and stones and the designer herself would often wear them – the designs supposedly based on her own real jewels. Alongside the little black dress and the quilted handbag, pearls have become synonymous with Chanel.

Costume jewellery has origins in the 18th century, when, it is thought, the wealthy feared travelling with their expensive jewellery for security reasons, but by the 1920s it had become a form of jewellery in its own right. Costume jewellery is also sometimes referred to as fashion jewellery – a term thought to have been coined in the 1980s and usually associated with more expensive costume jewellery.

Costume jewelley often takes inspiration from prevailing fashion trends, and dominant materials tend not to be high-end metals and precious stones, but rather plastics or resin. Much costume jewellery is collectible in its own right, though.

The condensed idea
A reflection of tradition, custom, function and fashion

43 The Corset

Judy Garland, as Esther Smith in the 1904-set film *Meet Me in St Louis* (1944), wonders whether she can be sensational and alluring without the corset she has just been tied and vigorously tightened into. Holding the bedpost, her sister tugs at the laces as Garland's character takes a big breath, feels faint, finds her feet and reassesses her new silhouette. A tiny waist. She agrees that she does feel elegant, as her sister points out she will, but cannot actually breathe.

> You can shape your waist with corsetry and it creates a feminine silhouette. It's not meant to be comfortable.
>
> Dita Von Teese

Being unable to breathe was a standard symptom of wearing a corset. Primarily seen as a symbol of discomfort and repression for women, this undergarment was worn mostly from the 16th–20th centuries to shape the body. It is still worn today, popular on red carpets and as a going-out top, but is now made using more comfortable fabrics and constructions for the wearer, with stretch built in. The biggest difference is that what was once an undergarment is now a standalone fashion garment.

In the beginning

Since its invention, the corset has been worn by both men and women and appeared as early as the Minoan civilization (c. 1600 BCE), where the first evidence of corsetlike garments are found in its art – women depicted wearing metal plates slimming the waist and emphasizing the bust. Garments that shape the waist also appeared during the Middle Ages in Europe.

It is the aristocracy who were first associated with corset-wearing, but bourgeois women were wearing them by the 18th century and women of lower classes would make their own, fashioning them from reeds for the support element. The corset fell out of fashion after the French Revolution as the empire line, which sat just under the bust, took hold. But they would reappear in the early 1800s as a trend for the waist in its natural position made it a part of a women's wardrobe once more. With the introduction of the sewing machine, corsets became more accessible to all classes.

Corsets of the 19th century were inspired by the 15th-century bodice, a close-fitting item made of two layers of linen that were sewn together for stiffness. In the 16th century, corsets were supported by rods to create a rigid front panel. Typically, corsets either laced up at the front or the back, with a decorative panel called a stomacher to cover up the laces on those that did so on the front. Before the 19th century, they were also called stays.

Shape up

The corset's primary purpose was to shape the body, moulding the upper body into a V-shape with a severely nipped-in waist, and flattening and pushing up the breasts to create a very pronounced silhouette. The shape a corset would create depended on the fashions of the time – the S-bend silhouette became popular towards the end of the 19th century, for example. Here, the corset extended over the hips and was cut low on the bust so that, when it was tightly laced, it narrowed the waist and pushed the bust and bottom out. It did not look comfortable to wear, such was the exaggerated and protruded shape, which was often accompanied by a bustle.

The corset's shaping capabilities would change. Cut longer in the early 20th century, to cover the thighs and create a straight figure, by the 1920s, a more gamine and natural silhouette prevailed, so corsets were worn less; they became more flexible with less boning in their design. However, restrictive dressing was not on the agenda of the era's flapper. There was a move again towards the hour-glass silhouette in the 1930s, but it would be Christian Dior who brought back the corset via his New Look.

The 20th-century corset

Eventually, as the 20th century progressed and clothes became more practical and modern for women, the corset was abandoned in favour of the brassiere, or bra, though it would remain as an element of bridalwear. Several designers, notably Vivienne Westwood, Jean Paul Gaultier, Thierry Mugler and Dolce & Gabbana, adopted the garment in their high-fashion collections (it is considered a signature of them all), often challenging

I did this corset, because people hadn't seen the décolletage for two hundred years.
Vivienne Westwood

Health issues

Corsets were the subject of great controversy. In 1850, protest groups formed to complain about the physical damage the tight lacing caused as it placed extreme pressure on the stomach. Women would often faint, and could potentially develop digestive, lung and reproductive issues because of the corset. In 1881, the Rational Dress Society formed in London. Members wore Turkish trousers and for health reasons would not wear fashion that restricted the body. Designers including Paul Poiret, Chanel, Lucile and Vionnet were among several who rejected the corset. Practical dressing took over at the turn of the 20th century and mirrored movement in society that made women more visible and called for their enfranchisement. By 1918, having been mobilized in war efforts, women over the age of 30 were now enfranchised in Britain.

its repressive connotations to present visions of powerful, empowered and liberated women, less than 100 years since it had conveyed the very opposite.

Westwood began using the corset in the mid-1980s, with collections such as Harris Tweed, Britain Must Go Pagan, Time Machine, Portrait, and War and Peace, which plundered the historical archives to put heaving bosoms back in fashion – this time as outerwear – and therefore subverting their original purpose. Using modern and more comfortable fabrics, Westwood is thought to have reclaimed women's power and freedom in her use of the garment. Thanks to the late designer's popularity on TikTok, corsets have once again become a favourite of Gen Z in the early 2020s.

The French designer, Jean Paul Gaultier, is one of the most influential designers in fashion and during the 1980s recreated the corset as outerwear, adding the bullet bra points of the 1950s to create the iconic cone shape that was worn by Madonna on her world tours. The designer is well known for challenging fashion ideas and provoking without offence. Instead there is wit, charm and humour to his designs.

Thierry Mugler established his label in the 1970s. The French designer was known for a confident and bold style that looked to the cinched silhouettes of the 1940s and 1950s, including corsets, which, under the direction of the American creative director Casey Cadwallader is upheld today.

The Italian design duo Domenico Dolce and Stefano Gabbana, known for their blend of Sicilian style and sexiness, have also made the corset a key part of their repertoire since the 1990s. In recent collections, they have incorporated them into their menswear offering, as well as teaming up with the social media/reality TV star Kim Kardashian, who is also well known for her controversial use of waist trainers, to create a collection in which it is worn over T-shirts for a modern spin.

The condensed idea
Empowering or imprisoning?

44 Trousers

Defined as an outer garment that, through two separate leg sections, covers the body from the waist or hips to the ankle and is known in a great number of different styles, shapes, lengths, cuts, fabrications and designs. Trousers are among the most complicated items to get right, be it by fit, make or aesthetics, and yet trousers, or pants as they are known in the United States, have been worn across the world in one form or another – by men, at least – since ancient times.

In 2014, a group of archaeologists discovered what is thought to be the oldest pair of trousers in the world, dated to around 3,000–3,300 years ago. Made from wool, they were found during the excavation of a tomb in the Tarim Basin of western China. They were on the mummified body of a man, but dated to a time when men and women were believed to have worn skirts and capes, so it is thought that they had been worn for horse riding.

Early-19th-century breeches, pantaloons and knickerbockers are the closest relation to trousers that we know today – all similarly short styles of trouser that were typically fitted to the knee. It is then, from the early 1800s, that straight, ankle-length trousers began to appear, which have undergone various updates ever since.

Who is wearing the trousers?

Trousers were once highly gendered, worn almost exclusively by men until the early 20th century in the Western world. On the rare occasions that women adopted them, they were seen as scandalous and immoral. Some fashion historians highlight the trouser as being the most significant advancement for women in the 20th century, pointing out that women's changing role in modern society – such as participating in sport and in the world of work through industrialization and war – made it acceptable for them to wear the same sort of dress as men. The events of World War II, for example, saw women adopting trousers when they took over the work of men in factories and fields; they were obviously more practical to wear than skirts.

Although it is generally acknowledged that skirts were worn almost exclusively until the end of the 1930s, the concept of trousers for

When someone asks: 'Who wears the trousers?', they want to know who is in control. Trousers, in this instance, represent power and authority, which, through history, have been bestowed on men. This is why, when women started wearing trousers, they were perceived as a threat.

women had been explored some years earlier – in particular, in 1851, when Amelia Jenks Bloomer promoted the bifurcated skirt. In the mid-1850s, Bloomer is reported to have been impressed by an article that suggested the shorter skirts and ankle-length trousers worn by Turkish women were more pragmatic than the skirts of women in Europe and America. Her design of baggy, Turkish-style trousers gathered at the ankle with a calf-length skirt worn over the top was adopted by women's rights advocates. Trousers became a symbol of freedom, power and independence.

Harem pants, meanwhile, were also based on trousers worn by Turkish women and appeared as a fashion around 1911, in a collection presented by designer Paul Poiret. The Ballets Russes made them popular in Europe in the early 1900s. Worn as eveningwear in the early 20th century, they became very popular in the 1930s.

Evolution

Actress Sarah Bernhardt is noted for wearing trousers in the late 19th century, though they were not commonly worn by women until the 1920s and 1930s – notably when Coco Chanel introduced 'yachting pants' and baggy styles of trouser that could be worn for the beach – 'beach pyjamas' – as well as leisure activities. By 1939, *Vogue* was advocating trousers with the instruction that a wardrobe was not complete without a great pair of tailored slacks – slacks being a semi-formal kind of trouser, one that is not part of a suit.

The 1960s saw a trouser-wearing revolution during a time when unisex dressing emerged and attitudes towards sex and gender were starting to shift. Of course, at the opposite end of the spectrum was the mini-skirt, which revealed the legs and caused just as much outcry. Trousers remained controversial until the 1970s; women wearing them were often refused entry to restaurants and certainly could not enter the Royal Enclosure at Royal Ascot. In 2013, the French government overturned a 200-year-old ban on women wearing trousers, imposed in 1800 – not that women had adhered to it for some time.

The trouser suit

Made famous in the 1930s by the actress, Marlene Dietrich, the women's trouser suit became iconic in the hands of Yves Saint Laurent. Known for challenging gender norms, the designer introduced Le Smoking in the 1960s. A precursor to the power dressing of the 1980s, this tuxedo-style suit offered trousers as an alternative to eveningwear, and was considered shocking at the time.

> I wanted women to have the same basic wardrobe as a man. Blazer, trousers and suit.
>
> Yves Saint Laurent

The American socialite Nan Kempner was famously refused entry at Le Côte Basque in hers; she promptly removed the trousers to wear her blazer as a minidress.

Ambassadors

Marlene Dietrich appropriated a great deal of male dress, including trousers, which she wore on screen, in her private life and during publicity shoots. Also in the 1930s and 1940s, actress Katharine Hepburn was known for wearing high-waisted, wide-leg trousers, which she accompanied with flat brogues. In 1969, Illinois congresswoman Charlotte Reid became the first woman to wear trousers in Congress – they were bell-bottoms. And the singer MC Hammer made baggy drop-crotch pants a signature during the 1980s.

Designers to know

Modern-day designers who had a considerable impact on the way we wear trousers are Hedi Slimane and Thom Browne. The former designed skinny styles while he was creative director at Dior Homme in the early 2000s. So loved were they by the late Karl Lagerfeld of Chanel, that he went on a diet in order to be able to wear them. The latter popularized, now ubiquitous, cropped, breakless-style trousers, part of a shrunken suit, during the early 2000s.

One leg or two?

Throughout the decades, designers have experimented with the idea of a one-legged trouser, but it has not caught on, appearing too avant-garde. In 2019, designers including Wesley Harriott, PushButton and VFiles put forward options that some younger style titles seemed to approve of.

Alexander McQueen, meanwhile, had experimented with a very revealing and daring 'bumster' style of trouser back in 1993. It showed off the top part of the posterior in a builders-bum sort of way, though the designer said it was about elongating the figure.

The condensed idea
A huge breakthrough in women's fashion

45 High Heels

The stiletto heel was invented in the 1950s. But the high heel's history dates back considerably further, centuries even, as a form of riding footwear circa the 15th or 16th century. That might seem surprising, given that the wearing of high heels is largely associated with impracticality, pain and discomfort today.

And yet it was high heels' pragmatism that made them so popular in the first place – pertinently with men, not women. Soldiers throughout western Asia wore heeled footwear to hold their feet in stirrups as good horsemanship was required for fighting in Persia, now Iran. The heels would secure the soldier while he set about firing his bow and arrow.

Such heels found their way to Europe when Persia's Shah Abbas I sent over a diplomat to establish ties with western Europe (in a bid to defeat the Ottoman Empire), which prompted a keen interest in all things Persian, among them heels. Aristocratic men adopted them, believing they reinforced their masculinity.

The trend filtered down to the lower strata of society and so to disassociate from them, the aristocrats increased their heel height (a standard algorithm when it comes to trends).

Status

It has been pointed out that these new shoes did not have a utility in the muddy streets of 17th-century Europe, but that was the idea. Impractical attire is a hallmark of high status, ultimately showing off luxury and privilege (vertiginous heels are frequently worn on red

Right of passage

High heels have anecdotally become a symbol of womanhood, growing up and maturity. Many high-heel aficionados talk about discovering their mother's heels when they were children and slipping their feet into them.

carpets today, their wearers safe in the knowledge that there is only the distance between the car and publicity shot spot to walk in them).

King Louis XIV of France – who is rumoured to have been around 163cm (5ft 4in) tall – was a particular fan of these new heels. And the soles of his were always red (a signature of the luxury footwear brand Christian Louboutin today). In the 1670s, Louis XIV restricted the wearing of such scarlet-soled shoes to those in his court alone, so they became a signifier of royal approval, superiority and nobility.

> High heels are a complete invention, an extravagance. They're far from natural, but it's the impracticality that I adore.
>
> Christian Louboutin

Soon, it would not just be lower-class men who took to wearing high heels but also women, as a trend for unisex fashion started to emerge, say historians, with women working out ways to make themselves more masculine. As a result, women started to wear high heels, whereas men started to adopt a more rational sense of dress. Men's shoes became squarer, lower and more practical.

During the Age of Enlightenment, in the 17th and 18th centuries, ideas regarding education and intellect played out in fashion. General attitudes towards women, it should be noted, saw them as being too emotional and irrational – attributes that men did not want to be associated with by wearing the same thing. What became known as the Great Masculine Renunciation (also known as the Great Male Renunciation) saw men sobering up their style. They stopped wearing jewellery and, by 1740, they had also stopped wearing high heels.

Some commentators note that high heels remained largely absent – for men and women – until the birth of photography and, with it, pornography in the mid-19th century. Nude women posed in high-heel shoes, which is why they also have associations with the erotic.

Hollywood also played a role in making high heels popular, sexy and glamorous; movie pin-ups and screen stars wore them and the world watched and copied. Film noir's protagonists proffered a sense of intrigue and mystery in their high heels, as viewers heard them running off down an alleyway. Supremely vertiginous heels in patent leather, with spikes and buckles, have become part of a fetish wardrobe, while the stiletto is a core part of the power-dressing uniform, thought to bring confidence.

In shoemaking, the heel is the part of the shoe that elevates the back of the foot. Heels can be high, medium or flat, as well as kitten, stiletto, Cuban, wedge and platform.

The chopine was a wooden or cork clog style, rather like an overshoe, worn during the 16th and 17th century, most notably in Venice. It was a raised platform that could reach lofty heights, worn rather like stilts under the skirts of the time to keep them, and shoes, safe from muddy street splatters.

Health issues

Criticism of high heels concerns how they change posture, forcing the wearer into an unnatural position and therefore impacting the spine. Bunions can also be a symptom of wearing high heels, as well as blisters (reportedly, in 2016, women bought more trainers than heels for the first time. And, during the pandemic, heels took a backseat for most as working from home meant loungewear was the daily outfit for many). Accidents can also happen: the supermodel, Naomi Campbell, famously took a tumble in a pair of platform high heels by Vivienne Westwood during the designer's 1993 catwalk. Luckily, she was able to laugh it off, but for many, this is a small price to pay for wearing some of the most stylish shoes around.

Famous fans

Arguably, Barbie has to be the most famous high-heel wearer, her feet pre-fashioned since 1959 with a high arch ready to slip them on whatever the outfit. In 2015, however, Mattel released a version with articulated ankles enabling her to get with the times and wear sneakers and gladiator sandals. The second most famous wearer has to be Sarah Jessica Parker's Carrie Bradshaw from *Sex and The City*, who was never seen without a pair of high heels as she ran around New York City during the early 2000s, making household names out of Manolo Blahnik and

> By now I can run a marathon in a pair of Manolo Blahnik heels.
>
> Sarah Jessica Parker, *Manolo Blahnik Drawings*

Jimmy Choo. Since then, fashion designers, footwear designers and houses have played around with the high heel, switching the standard stiletto or spike shapes for altogether more surreal suggestions such as tubular steel frames (Paco Rabanne via Julien Dossena), roses (Loewe) and logos (Yves Saint Laurent).

The condensed idea
Men wore them first

46 The Trench Coat

Among the design classics heralded in fashion, the trench coat is unanimously one of them. What started out as a utilitarian design intended for weather and war became an icon of fashion, timeless and chic, worn by everyone from Audrey Hepburn – in *Breakfast at Tiffany's* (1961), there is perhaps no less iconic moment – and Marlene Dietrich, Greta Garbo, Catherine Deneuve to Inspector Clouseau and Columbo.

> I know personally I can't live without a good pair of jeans, a trench coat, weird shoes, a tiny handbag and my contact lenses.
> Alexa Chung

Known for its practicalities as well as its femme fatale allure, the trench became a unisex garment suitable for businessmen, flashers and spies, so popular culture tells it. Just as with sportswear, while it did not start out as a fashion item, the design soon made the transition in the wake of World War I. Innovation lies in a handful of names: Burberry, Aquascutum and Mackintosh.

Trench coat or mac?

Fashion dictionaries define both the mac, or Mackintosh, and the trench as a type of waterproof coat. The latter, a 19th-century military style coat with epaulets and a double yoke at its shoulders, is often attributed to Thomas Burberry. The two are very similar in appearance and, though they have become interchangeable in 20th-century civilian life, each has its own story to tell.

Burberry

Thomas Burberry was a shop owner born in Dorking, Surrey, England, who trained as an apprentice to a draper. In 1856, he opened his own business, T Burberry & Sons, in Basingstoke, Hampshire. So one story goes, in collaboration with a cotton mill, Burberry produced a waterproof coat based on the style of an agricultural smock. The cotton cloth was gabardine, a durable and waterproof fabric. The brand had been founded on the premise that clothing should be designed to protect people from the British weather. Burberry notes that gabardine was invented in 1879 and patented in 1888.

Across the film noir genre, trench coats have played a starring role, imbuing a character with a sense of intrigue and mystery. All the best detectives have worn them, making it a spy staple, and a great equalizer. Hollywood's leading ladies wore the trench coat off-screen as well as on. Dietrich made it her signature, while Sophia Loren, Marilyn Monroe, Jane Birkin and Brigitte Bardot all tried it on for size. Humphrey Bogart wore one in the iconic *Casablanca* (1942), cementing its association with wartime.

Later, businessmen across the generations were taken seriously because of the coat's practical credentials and smart, belted and put-together appearance – the perfect accompaniment to the leather briefcase.

During World War I, Burberry introduced its trench coat, a functional design that included epaulettes, D-rings and the storm shield. The military style of the Burberry trench coat became that of the war. After the war, the trench coat was absorbed into daily life, often worn by women during the 1940s. According to the brand, it takes a year for each specialist tailor to learn the stitching of the trench collar alone. And there are more than 180 stitches required to create its fluid curves that make it sit just right on the neck.

Mackintosh

The Mackintosh is a waterproof coat that was developed in various stages of the 19th century, starting in 1823 when Scottish chemist Charles Mackintosh patented a waterproof woollen fabric. The material is still named after him. Sixteen years later, American Charles Goodyear introduced vulcanized rubber, while Joseph Mandleburg, from the United Kingdom, was responsible for launching the first odour-free waterproof coat in 1851. The first macs of the late 19th century were said to be voluminous shapes and designed specifically to keep the wearer completely dry. Just as the trench coat became adopted by civilians, so too did the Mackintosh as it became a fashionable style.

Aquascutum

Meaning 'water shield' in Latin, Aquascutum was established in 1851 as a tailor's shop in London by John Emary. Aquascutum developed showerproof coats made from wool, which were worn by British soldiers in the trenches during World War I. They were ankle length with epaulets and brass rings on the belt.

As well as supplying coats for the military, between the wars, Aquascutum sold showerproof coats to men and women, catering to the increasingly outdoor lifestyles they were living. From the 1950s, coats were reportedly made from a cotton and nylon poplin called Wyncol D.711, and in 1955, new shades of cotton gaberdine came along. Up until this point they had been available primarily in grey, blue and beige. That same year, they further broke with tradition and shortened their coats to the knee.

Evolution

The trench coats of World War I were typically double-breasted, tailored to the waist and flared below the knee. A belt featured D-rings for accessories and a caped back allowed water to drip off, while a storm flap provided ventilation. The term first appeared in print, it is thought, in 1916, in a tailoring trade journal. Epaulettes indicated rank and the colours issued were typically khaki for camouflage. Post-war trench coats took on beige and camel tones and became less bulky.

The trench coat has been a mainstay of wardrobes for decades, and designers have experimented with the garment season on season, changing length and colour, details and stitching, deconstructing and remaking, and leaning either into its military heritage or erasing it altogether. Recent examples of designers who have chopped it up, reworked it and played with proportions include Balenciaga, Sacai and Balmain for autumn/winter 2024. In 2019, Japanese designer Junya Watanabe experimented with the item to turn it into a dress, among other items. Time and again, it does seem to be a garment that designers are curious to experiment with – including Burberry. Under the creative direction of Christopher Bailey, the brand sent out

Mackintosh's signature rubberized coats continue to be made by skilled craftsmen in the same tradition pioneered in the early 19th century.

mackintosh.com

versions to all sorts of themes: they came lace embellished and bejewelled, romantic and whimsical, sharp and powerful.

The condensed idea
From war wear to
modern wardrobe

47 The Little Black Dress

Few items of clothing have their own universally acknowledged acronym but LBD, for the little black dress, is one of them. It is a design classic, simple yet elegant, and with the ability to look smart and dressed up but not over the top. It has a uniform quality to it but can equally be customized as a black canvas on which to show off jewellery and accessories.

The LBD officially emerged during the 1920s and was based on a chemise with its simple lines. But that is not to say that black dresses did not exist before then (black is noted as already being a popular colour), and Chanel, who helped popularize the LBD, had begun showing black dresses around 1913. Further, it was popular in the 1930s and has become a mainstay in the modern wardrobe for women. It is easy and uncomplicated.

> It's about the democratization, mass production and modernization of women's dress.
>
> Georgina Ripley, curator

Often, but not always, cut to show the shoulders and the arms, the LBD was ideally suited to cocktail hour, a 1920s US invention that ran between 6pm and 8pm. While, today, anyone can walk into any shop and find a little black dress to wear, there are various designers who specifically helped to promote it and to whom it is attributed as their design.

Chanel

Gabrielle Chanel, responsible for so many of fashion's inventions, specialized in designs that were light and easy to wear and did not need to involve a corset. In her designing of the LBD, she democratized elegance, just as she had democratized so many aspects of life for women with her clothes.

In 1926, American *Vogue* compared her LBD design, thought to be a day dress with long sleeves, to the Ford Model T car, which is generally regarded as being the first mass-affordable automobile, debuting in 1908. By saying this, they meant it could be worn by all women whatever their economic status. It became a fashion staple and therefore also had a utilitarian appeal, and notably it was released to the backdrop of the Great Depression.

Hard to wear?

The LBD is said to be one of the easiest things to wear but, as Diana Vreeland pointed out, black is the hardest colour to get right.

Edward Molyneux

During the 1920s and 1930s, British designer Edward Molyneux promoted the LBD. He was known for his fine lines, as well as the cut of his tailoring and bias-cut dresses. Born in London, Molyneux studied art and began his career sketching for magazines. He was subsequently hired by Lady Duff Gordon, of the English couture maison Lucile, to work in her salon. Travelling with her to Paris, New York and Chicago, he opened a dressmaking shop in Paris after World War I, further branches of which were opened in Monte Carlo, Cannes, Biarritz and London.

Givenchy and Audrey Hepburn

Among the most famous LBDs is that worn by Holly Golightly, played by Audrey Hepburn, in Blake Edwards's *Breakfast at Tiffany's* (1961). French designer Hubert de Givenchy designed the iconic dress, which memorably appears in the opening scene, with Hepburn getting out of a cab on Fifth Avenue, pastry and coffee in hand and her eye caught by the window of Tiffany's, the fine jeweller. She is decked out in glittering pearls herself, which sit atop the simple but striking design.

Givenchy's LBD is fitted, nipped at the waist and has a petal-shaped longer length skirt, slit to the thigh on one side. At its back, it shows off the shoulder blades with a distinctive cut-out décolleté. In 2006, the dress sold at auction at Christie's, accompanied by a pair of black elbow-length gloves. It had an estimate of £50–70,000 but actually realized £467,200. It is surely among the most famous of little black dresses, though there have been others to note.

The revenge dress

Diana, Princess of Wales, famously wore a black cocktail dress designed by Christina Stambolian to London's Serpentine Gallery in

Black is a significant colour because, up until this point, it had only been acceptable to wear it at funerals or as mourning dress. To wear black clothes outside of these situations was deemed inappropriate, but black would be the colour adopted by the hedonistic flapper girls of the 1920s, who would also partake in cocktail hour. What Chanel did was to break from tradition and make the colour a smart and chic choice, readily accepted for a new generation of women.

1994. An off-the-shoulder design, fitted and featuring a chiffon draping skirt, the royal wore it following the news that her then husband, Charles, Prince of Wales, had committed adultery. It was a show-stopping piece and to this day is among the best-known dresses in both popular culture and contemporary fashion history.

That dress

In 1994, the actress Elizabeth Hurley accompanied her then partner Hugh Grant to the premiere of *Four Weddings and a Funeral*. To it, she wore a little black dress of a different kind, one that ever since has been referred to as 'that' dress. Though longer in length than the average preconceived LBD, it was brief on the side and held together by giant decorative safety pins that flashed flesh between. It was the work of the Italian fashion house Versace.

Over the years

While less associated with the little black dress than his contemporaries, Christian Dior did his bit, designing demure cocktail dresses in black taffeta. By the 1960s, the fashion landscape would start to shift as the dawn of the Youthquake movement, underpinned by colour, made the little black dress seem conservative.

The 1970s also explored prints and patterns, colour and a move towards more casual dressing – flares and maxi skirts spring to mind more than little black dresses. It would be the 1980s that picked them back up as body-conscious silhouettes and power dressing became fashionable. And, during the 1990s, the era of supermodels, designers such as Dolce & Gabbana would put their stamp on the style – lingerie-like in svelte silhouettes. There would also be a grunge moment, where the chemise style the LBD was originally based on was teamed with Doc Marten boots for a rebellious take on the democratic classic.

The little black dress has appeared throughout the decades in various incarnations. Its status as a classic means it will never be in or out of fashion, but it will always be there, safe, reliable, elegant and sexy – depending on what style the wearer selects.

The condensed idea
A design classic

48 The Bra

The bra is one of fashion's more socio-political items of dress, or undress, highly associated with women's liberation (and, for some, the lack of it). This relatively contemporary item only really dates back to just over 100 or so years ago in the form we know it today. This might seem surprising given that the bra industry is estimated to be worth $59.5 billion by 2032.

Widely reported, though, is the 'bikini girl' mosaic at the Villa Romana del Casale in Sicily, which depicts a series of young women in bandeau-style tops (though, it seems, no straps), while they apparently do some sort of sport. It is dated to the 4th century CE. After that, there seems to be quite a lull before we get to the invention of the bra. There are various developments in undergarments, including the bra's predecessor, the corset, but the job of the corset was more to shape the body than it was to shape or support the breasts. And that is where the bra stepped in, evolving as women's visibility and place in society has grown. As women became more mobile in an increasingly pragmatic and industrialized world, fashions changed to reflect this. And the prohibitive nature of the corset required a rethink.

Just like the corset, the bra is reflective of attitudes to gender, sex, morality and power. It is an undergarment that, looking back, has typically been able to pinpoint what, overarchingly, is in fashion: breast-flattening bandeaus were worn by the perceived scandalous and rebellious flappers of the 1920s; the 1950s were about pronounced, very feminine hourglass points; and a vogue for going bra-less came in the new and youthful 1960s and 1970s. Depending on the context, bras can be considered a badge of modernity and conformity, but also a symbol of feminism and femininity.

Innovation

The word 'bra' was shortened from the French *brassiere*, which is thought to have first been used for the garment in 1905. Its aim was to support, and at times, to shape the breasts via two cups held in place by straps and an elastic back. The US socialite Mary Phelps Jacob is credited with developing the first modern bra around 1913 or 1914, and she did so under a pseudonym, Caresse Crosby. Hers was a

Bra trivia

Apparently, film director Howard Hughes had a specially designed bra made for the actress Jane Russell in *The Outlaw* (1943) but she didn't wear it because it was too uncomfortable. Bras are not easy to make. Indeed, the storied brand Rigby & Peller notes its own require 40 components, and fashion colleges today offer specialized courses in the making of lingerie. Notably, statistics published in the past decade suggest 80 per cent of women are wearing the wrong size – proving bras are a complicated subject.

boneless design, and she sold the patent to lingerie manufacturers Warner Brothers Corset Company.

It was in the 1930s that the bra is thought to have acquired the attributes it still features today, including letter sizing for cups, the hook-and-eye fastenings and the adjustable straps. Various developments in its production – from colour to material – as well as the promotion of it on the silver screen helped it to go mainstream.

The bullet bra, popular during the 1950s, was made up of layers of cotton with the cups stitched into concentric circles that moved outwards from the point of the bust. It is thought to have been the most rigid of undergarments in its construction since the corset and was prolific in advertising of the time.

Feminism and burning bras

Initially the bra became a symbol of modernity because it was less restricting than the corset, but as the 20th century progressed, bras, too, would come to be seen as restrictive. It was at a Miss America contest in 1968 that the bra-burning myth began. Protesting at the pageant in New Jersey, women threw lipsticks and high heels into what they called a 'freedom trash can', the idea being that they were throwing away symbols of oppression. One woman removed her bra and threw it in, a move that made headlines and became a feminist moment in history. The idea of the bra-burning feminist had been born. Though no bras were apparently ever actually set on fire, according to those involved, the concept has stuck and is associated as being a branch of feminism.

Underwear as outerwear in fashion

The bra was intended as a female undergarment, but by the late 20th century, fashion designers had started to explore the idea of underwear as outerwear. Provocative when it first took a turn on the catwalk, this is now a recurring theme in fashion.

In 1982, Vivienne Westwood debuted the Buffalo Girls collection, which featured satin bras worn on the outside of looks. Meanwhile Jean Paul Gaultier introduced the iconic pointy conical shape that was used on his bra designs in 1983 – later used on a belted corset version and worn by Madonna for her Blond Ambition tour in 1990. It sold at auction in 2012 for $52,000. The French designer has explained that he first made the conical bra for his teddy bear when he was a child. It would become a trademark of his, seen in many collections thereafter.

Bras would be used by many other fashion designers besides, and in recent years they have become a major trend in fashion, worn on many a catwalk and many a red carpet.

The WonderBra

Frederick's of Hollywood, established in 1946, has been credited with inventing the first push-up bra, called the Rising Star. The concept is also synonymous with WonderBra. In 1939, Moses Nadler founded the Canadian Lady Corset Company and licensed the WonderBra trademark. In 1960, it launched a push-up bra under the WonderBra trademark, followed by a plunge push-up bra in 1963. It became a best-seller and was licensed to brands in Europe to sell. The design took off in the United Kingdom during the 1970s.

In 1994, along came the very impactful 'Hello Boys' campaign in the United States, which featured the supermodel, Eva Herzigova, in her bra. In 1998, actress Adriana Karembeu succeeded Herzigova as face of the campaign. It was a provocative campaign that prompted both criticism and praise. The brand has since experimented with T-shirt bras and wireless styles – the opposite to what made it famous – as it has moved with the times.

Famous bras

Madonna is likely among the most famous bra-wearers owing to her relationship with Jean Paul Gaultier, but singers Gwen Stefani, Lady Gaga and Rihanna are also fans. The last has her own lingerie brand, Savage X Fenty. Other notable bra moments in time include Victoria's Secret, the underwear brand known for its extravagant catwalk shows in which bras become part of butterfly outfits, and the Fembots in *Austin Powers: Man of Mystery* (1997), who used theirs as weapons.

The condensed idea
A sign of modernity

49 The Bikini

Diana Vreeland, the late, great editor-in-chief of *Vogue* and fashion editor of *Harper's Bazaar*, and known for her many great fashion quotes, is famous for saying that the bikini was the most important thing since the atom bomb, giving just a hint of its explosive nature.

When the bikini first entered fashion's consciousness, it had been little more than 50 years since bustles had been in fashion, with layers of skirts being standard day-to-day attire – the very idea of showing off skin was shocking.

Jacques Heim, a French couturier, and Louis Réard, a Swiss engineer and a lesser-known designer, have both been credited with inventing the bikini, doing so at the same time, but working separately. Their two-piece bathing suits originated in 1946, in France – though pre-Code Hollywood films of the early 1930s did show midriff-bearing swimsuits. (The 'Code' in pre-Code comes from the American Hays Code (1934), a series of guidelines prohibiting suggestive nudity and realistic violence in film.) There are differing stories on exactly how the bikini got its

Miss World

For better or worse, bikinis are often associated with beauty pageants. In 1951, the Festival Bikini Contest was held in Britain – it would go on to become known as Miss World. The first winner, Kiki Hakansson, was crowned wearing a bikini. Controversy ensued, however, as Pope Pius XII said the swimsuit was sinful and it was reportedly banned from beauty pageants thereafter. Belgium, Portugal, Spain and Italy outlawed the item. And, as recently as 2022, Italy has further banned the bikini from certain places. The town of Sorrento said it would issue fines of 500 euros to anyone caught wearing one; the mayor said that bikini-wearing and topless tourists made the locals feel uncomfortable. The rule did not apply to people at beach clubs or swimming pools. Barcelona and Majorca also introduced fines for people that year if they were anywhere other than on the beach.

name: Heim reportedly called his bikini the *atome*, but it was later named after a nuclear weapons test that took place on a site called Bikini Atoll in the Pacific.

Two-piece swimsuits had begun to emerge as a result of World War II, owing to the rationing of goods, which included fabric. Iterations consisted of a more structured halter top and a bottom that covered up to the thigh. The bikini was first seen on the runway – that of Réard's – in Paris, on the French showgirl, Micheline Bernardini. In 1947, a green and white polka-dot bikini featured in the US edition of *Harper's Bazaar*, by the US sportswear designer Carolyn Schnurer.

In 1960, the bikini became the subject of the song 'Itsy Bitsy Teeny Weenie Yellow Polka-Dot Bikini' by Paul Vance and Lee Pockriss, and performed by Brian Hyland. It told the story of a shy woman in a revealing bikini who was afraid to come out of the locker and rather sums up the prevailing sentiment of the style at the time. They were already popular in France by the 1950s but were not so readily accepted by the United States until the mid-1960s.

Outrage!

Indeed, when it first debuted, the bikini, which showed off far more flesh than had been shown before, caused outcry. Displaying the wearer's navel, it was deemed both liberating and scandalous. It took a few more years, until the dawn of the 1960s, when clothes grew shorter and smaller in general, and a new attitude towards sex and the body took hold, for it to be more generally accepted.

There were also variations such as the string bikini, which came along in the 1970s. This consisted, just about, of two small triangles of fabric held together by ties at each hip and a bra-like top. There is also the tankini, more of a vest-style top and knickers.

Pin-up girls

Much like the bra, the bikini was popularized by 1950s pin-up girls, and a great number of film actresses of the 1960s and 1970s have had iconic film moments wearing a bikini, ultimately granting them a sex-symbol status. These include Brigitte Bardot in *And God Created Woman* (1956) and *The Girl In The Bikini* (1952); Raquel Welch in *One Million Years BC* (1966) and *Bedazzled* (1967); Ursula Andress in *Dr No* (1962); Sue Lyon in *Lolita* (1962); Honor Blackman in

The monokini

Probably the most avant-garde of all bikini designs is the monokini, which had mixed reactions from the press when it came out, but is thought to have sold in record numbers to consumers. The monokini was invented – and coined – by California-based designer Rudi Gernreich, and consisted of a topless swimsuit, which was taboo-breaking at the time.

Gernreich designed the piece for both men and women and was keen to promote unisex ideas of dressing. The earliest prototype appeared in 1962 and went on sale in 1964. The item was never actually intended for swimming in as it was knitted from water-bearing wool. The designer also developed the 'no bra' bra in 1964 and became known for his sportswear and knitted jersey tube dresses, but will forever be remembered for his quirky approach to swimwear.

Goldfinger (1964); Jayne Mansfield in *Panic Button* (1964); Trina Parks in *Diamonds are Forever* (1971); Pam Grier in *Coffy* (1973); Gloria Hendry in *Live and Let Die* (1972); Carrie Fisher in *Star Wars* (1977); and Halle Berry in *Die Another Day* (2002).

Among the most famous bikinis in pop culture are Raquel Welch's fur bikini, used for the promotional adverts for *One Million Years BC*, and Carrie Fisher's gold bikini worn when she played Princess Leia in *Star Wars Return of the Jedi* (1983). In 2015, the latter sold for £63,000 at auction. The costume also included a collar and several chain links and a letter of authenticity.

Style

Bikini designs have evolved over the years, getting bigger, smaller and more, or less, ostentatious. Much like the bra, they have also reflected attitudes towards women. Early bikini designs tended to be trimmed and decorated with animal motifs and flowers. Sometimes they were made from crochet. By the 1990s, bikinis were readily accepted in fashion, on the beach and at the pool, and as the vogue for tanning and waxing became popular, the bikini became the best way to show this off.

In 1997, Miss America, for the first time in its history, allowed bikinis during the swimsuit portion of the contest – though it would get rid of this category in the contest altogether in 2018. The early noughties saw the introduction of a fashion week dedicated to swimwear, Miami Swim Week, where bikinis play a huge role.

Recent years have seen a return to the fashion for showing off the bust and bikinis have become smaller than ever. In 1996, the then creative director of Chanel, Karl Lagerfeld, had shown a microkini at the brand's spring/summer show. In 2022, the actress Jennifer Aniston wore Lagerfeld's microkini on the front cover of *Allure* magazine.

The condensed idea
Outrageous, yet groundbreaking

50 The Mini-Skirt

An icon of the 1960s and early 1970s, the mini-skirt debuted two decades after Christian Dior's New Look, which was characterized by glamorous, stylized proportions, splaying dirndl skirts and nipped-in waists. In contrast, the mini-skirt was just as the name implies: short, androgynous and showing off plenty of leg. It was a badge of modernity and sexual liberation in the wake of 1950s traditions and ushered in a futuristic era that centred on a new generation: the Youthquake.

The 1960s was a decade of remarkable change and advance. In 1961, Soviet Yuri Gagarin became the first man in space and Ham the chimp became the first ape in space. Meanwhile, back on planet Earth, a sci-fi makeover was taking place across fashion and design and a retail revolution was starting to take hold in London. In a post-war world full of teenagers, now obsessed with a new band called The Beatles, everyone was looking to the future, which seemed bright and colourful. Young shoppers revelled in the rise of the new independent boutiques in London and the exciting fashions they offered.

> It symbolized to those around them that times were changing and women were active and visible.
>
> Rebecca Arnold, historian

The mini-skirt was part of all of this. Its design is attributed to a handful of designers from the decade. They include the British Mary Quant and John Bates and the French André Courrèges and Pierre Cardin. The origins of the mini-skirt, however, can be traced back to ancient times and a traditional garment worn by the ancient Greeks and ancient Romans: the tunic. Throughout history, men have worn a tunic with leggings or tights.

Further, archaeologists have found figurines dating between 5400–4700 BCE dressed in kilt-like coverings. Egyptians wore the *schenti*, a cloth worn around the waist and secured by a belt. Women's legs, however, remained covered up for centuries, and often behind layers and layers of skirt. In modern times, it would not be until the beginning of the 20th century that hemlines were on the rise.

It was the 1920s that fashion first started to see a substantial change in hem length, though not yet to mini proportions. The flapper style

The fashion for the mini-skirt coincided with the commercial availability of the birth control pill in the early 1960s and the growing visibility of women in society as a result of the post-war world. Worn by feminists and young women alike, who wanted to reject the traditional gender rules, as well as the staid fashion styles worn by their mothers, it signified that women were active, and that attitudes to them in society were changing. It was comfortable to wear and did not restrict movement. It was also a world away from Victorian times and attitudes, when simply flashing an ankle was considered risqué.

of dress, with its straight-and-down shape, prompted a similar reaction of outrage to the mini-skirt when it emerged. Both were deemed scandalous and immoral for their implied promiscuity.

Measurements

The mini-skirt is defined by its micro proportions, which see it ending well above the knee. Skirts rose just above the knee in 1961 and had reached the upper thigh by 1966. There was also a microskirt, which just about covered the wearer's behind. Interestingly, the mini-skirt's rise in popularity seems to have chimed with a time that trousers started to become universal for women.

Mary Quant

So the story goes, Mary Quant officially introduced the mini-skirt in 1958, naming it after the Mini car, a model that became iconic during the 1960s. She said she had been influenced by the street style of London in the 1950s and 1960s, the latter soon to be known as the Swinging Sixties, which saw a move away from traditions of the past. Hemlines were on the rise, having been previously at the knee or below it. Quant attended Goldsmiths, in London, from 1950–53 and opened a boutique called Bazaar on King's Road, where she sold designs geared towards this younger market, known as the Chelsea Look. It was about a silhouette that enabled freedom and had

The Swinging Sixties was a youth-driven culture revolution; its capital was London. Geared towards modernity, change, music and fashion, it launched the careers of models and musicians such as Twiggy, Jean Shrimpton, The Rolling Stones, The Kinks and The Beatles. In 1965, the grand dame of fashion, Diana Vreeland, editor of the then powerful American *Vogue*, declared London to be the world's most exciting city.

been largely inspired by the simple lines of children's clothing, as well as its colour palette.

John Bates

Bates was a designer and costume designer from Northumberland, in England. After stints working at Herbert Siddon, then as a freelance illustrator and working in wholesale – and, at one point, for Quant – he is also linked to the mini-skirt revolution, credited with introducing some of the shortest minidresses of the early 1960s. He would not be the only one.

André Courrèges

Courrèges, born in France, trained with the master designer Cristóbal Balenciaga, who was known for his structured but voluminous silhouettes, joining him in 1949. He opened his own house in 1961 and throughout the decade proffered very short skirts and minidresses with trousers, which was another way to wear the trend at the time. His designs were known for their sharp angles and sci-fi futuristic feel, giving him a reputation as a 'space-age' designer, which conveyed he was ahead of his time.

Pierre Cardin

Cardin, an Italian-French designer, left home at the age of 17 to work for a tailor in Vichy, making suits for women. In 1945, after the liberation of France, he went to work in Paris where he took jobs with Paquin and Schiaparelli; he also worked for Dior. During the 1950s,

Mini facts

Such was the appeal of the mini-skirt and what it symbolized, that a group calling themselves the British Society for the Protection of Mini Skirts protested outside the Dior show in 1966, when the fashion house showed longer hemlines on the runway.

Back in 1925, a bill introduced in Utah, in the United States, said that those who wore skirts shorter than 7.5cm (3in) above the ankle would be fined or imprisoned.

he produced collections for women and men, and by 1964 he produced a space-age collection and next came short skirts – with hemlines that were 10cm (4in) above the knee.

RIP, the mini-skirt

By the 1970s, the mini-skirt was on its way out as flowing hippy skirts and flared trousers were on their way in, signalling a new fashion moment of their own.

Power suits of the 1980s would see mini-skirts take on the boardroom, also immortalized in *Pretty Woman* (1990), when Julia Roberts wore hers with thigh-high boots, and they would wander in and out of fashion to no specific daring effect thereafter. Madonna, Cindi Lauper and Debbie Harry of Blondie have been among its ambassadors. But in the 2020s, they have gone even shorter, last spotted on the Miu Miu spring/summer 2022 catwalk as the micromini.

The condensed idea
Women's liberation

Glossary

Activewear Clothing made for physical activity or exercise, such as working out, that is comfortable and casual. Similar to sportswear, there is some crossover with garments such as leggings, vests and hoodies.

Athleisure A hybrid of athletic attire and leisure garments – and a combination of the two words – suitable to wear for both sports and everydaywear; eg hoodies and joggers. Considered to be a more stylish version of activewear or sportswear.

Blockchain A digital ledger used to record ownership and transactions of digital and real-life assets.

Breeches An early form of trouser that reached to below the knee; similar in style to the jodhpur.

Catwalk The walkway, sometimes raised, on which models walk to show off clothes at a fashion show.

Circular economy A system whereby materials never become waste and everything is, in one way, kept in circulation through methods such as recycling and composting.

Cowl neckline A draped neckline that is loose and gathered. It can be worn both low and plunging on an evening gown or high and wide on a jumper.

Décolleté Referring to the low-cut neckline on a dress or top that reveals the wearer's skin from bosom to neck.

Empire line Where the waistline is raised to being just under the bust. From ancient origins, it was popular during the First Empire in France (1804–14), the Regency era in Britain (1811–20) and again during the 1970s.

Gen alpha Term for those born typically between 2010 and 2024, a generation characterized as tending to be the children of millennials. This generation has likely been online since birth.

Gen Z Term for those born during the late 1990s and early 2000s, characterized by its diversity.

Glamazon Someone who is very glamorous, often tall, self-assured and confident. From 'glamorous' and 'Amazonian' combined.

Halterneck The neckline of a garment held up by one strap around the neck as opposed to two around the shoulders.

Ivy League Shorthand for elite aesthetics. Originally refers to an athletic sports conference of eight American universities including Harvard and Yale.

Leg-of-mutton sleeve The shape of a sleeve that is bulbous at the shoulder and top arm and shrinks down at the elbow to fit more tightly down to the wrist. Popular during the 1800s.

Letterman sweater Sweater, or jacket, adorned with the letter of a school's initial received upon outstanding achievement in sports or academia.

Maison A French term to refer to 'house', as in a fashion house. *Maison* in this instance typically conveys heritage and prestige.

Microskirt A shorter than average mini-skirt.

Net-a-Porter Founded by Natalie Massenet in 2000, one of the first designer e-commerce platforms focusing on luxury clothing and accessories.

Normcore A brief style movement (from the early to mid-2010s) centred on looking as everyday and pedestrian as possible.

Ode-to Positively inspired by something; giving a nod to it.

Peter-Pan collar Rounded collar flat in design, often worn by children, and taken from the costumes worn in Peter Pan.

Petit mains Meaning small hands, the term used to describe the haute-couture atelier artisans who physically create the garments.

Pleather A synthetic form of leather that can come in various makes, varieties and weights.

Prêt-à-porter French term meaning ready-to-wear and denoting mass-manufactured garments that can be sold in shops without any further alterations.

Runway American term for catwalk.

Ruff An elaborate wheel-like collar worn around the neck by men and women historically – most famously by Queen Elizabeth I of England (1533–1603).

Silhouette Used to describe the shape or outline of a garment.

Silkscreen A stencil-like process of printing in which colour is pressed onto the surface of a fabric through the mesh of a screen.

Skin A skin is a digital garment or hairstyle (or any personal effect) that is added to an in-game character, also known as an avatar, to change how it looks or acts.

Smart-casual An in-between and versatile form of dressing that enables the wearer to traverse both smart and formal or casual and informal situations. It is neither too dressed up or dressed down.

Supplement An accompanying magazine or piece of printed matter that goes with the main paper or magazine, either on a regular and seasonal, or one-off, basis.

Sweatshop In the clothing industry, a factory or workshop with poor conditions and pay for its workers.

Torque An ancient type of jewellery – a collar or a neckpiece featuring twisted metal that typically curves at the end to decorative effect, or to fasten. Can also be an armband or ring.

Trickle-down effect The term to describe how trends and ideas disseminate from a place of prestige and exclusivity down to a wider and more accessible market.

Tuxedo A type of smart, formal dinner suit that is often worn with a bowtie, whereas a regular suit may be worn with a tie.

Varsity jacket Another term for a letterman jacket, worn by elite athletes, often associated with the 1950s.

Waist trainer Similar to a girdle or a corset, it is a controversial garment that is supposed to help shrink the wearer's waist.

Zine A self-published and independent magazine that is often niche in subject matter and with a small circulation.

Index

About the author

Jessica Bumpus is a freelance journalist and formerly the Fashion Features Editor of British *Vogue* online. She studied at London College of Fashion, University of the Arts London, receiving a First in Fashion Promotion before joining Condé Nast. Her work has appeared in the *International New York Times*, the *Financial Times*, *The Week Fashion*, MarieClaire.co.uk, HarpersBazaar.com and *Elle* US, among others. She is author of *Vivienne Westwood, the Story Behind the Style* (2023) and *The Little Book of Dolce & Gabbana* (2024).

Greenfinch,
An imprint of Quercus Editions Ltd
Carmelite House
50 Victoria Embankment
London EC4Y 0DZ
An Hachette UK company

Published in 2024
Copyright © Jessica Bumpus

Jessica Bumpus asserted her right to be identified as the author of this Work.

All rights reserved. No part of this publication may be reproduced or transmitted in any form or by any means, electronic or mechanical, including photocopy, recording, or any information storage and retrieval system, without permission in writing from the publisher.

A CIP catalogue record for this book is available from the British Library

PB ISBN 9781529438376
eBook ISBN 9781529438383

Quercus Editions Ltd hereby exclude all liability to the extent permitted by law for any errors or omissions in this book and for any loss, damage or expense (whether direct or indirect) suffered by a third party relying on any information contained in this book.

SRD

Printed and bound in India by Manipal Technologies Limited, Manipal

MIX
Paper | Supporting responsible forestry
FSC™ C043100
www.fsc.org

Papers used by Greenfinch are from well-managed forests and other responsible sources.